The Far Land

EVA MACLEAN

The Caitlin Press
Prince George, British Columbia
1993

The Caitlin Press P.O. Box 2387, Station B Prince George, B.C. V2N 2S6 Canada

The Caitlin Press would like to acknowledge the financial support of the Canada Council and British Columbia Cultural Fund. Photos of the Hazelton bank robbery appear courtesy the British Columbia Archives and Records Service.

Canadian Cataloguing in Publication Data

MacLean, Eva, 1888-1984
The Far Land

isbn 0-920576-41-91

Hazelton (B.C.)—Biography. 2. Hazelton (B.C.)—History I. Title.
FC3849.H39Z48 1993   791.1'85   C93-091090-7
F1089.5.H39M32 1993

Cover Design by Kelly Brooks

Typeset by The Vancouver Desktop Publishing Centre Ltd.

Printed in Canada

Contents

Foreword

The voices from history are almost always those of men. The politicians, railway tycoons, urban promoters, and religious leaders tended to be males — at least those are the people who spoke the loudest and wrote the most about their exploits and contributions. One has to listen carefully for women's voices, to hear traces of the stories, experiences, and memories of the females who lived in the north in decades past. And then, often unexpectedly, a new voice emerges, one not before heard, offering a different perspective on events that we thought we knew well.

Eva MacLean — wife, mother, music teacher, entertainer, and story-teller — has added her name to that short but important list of northern British Columbians who have recounted their life experiences and thus ensured that the lessons of the past are not lost forever. Her story is a modest one, told with a gentleness of spirit and sprightly humour, that nonetheless reveals the hardship and excitement, sadness, and pleasure of life in north central British Columbia in the second decade of this century.

Mrs. MacLean's recollections span an important period in the history of the northern interior — the years immediately before and during World War I, when the Grand Trunk Pacific Railway was being built across the province. The coming of the railway brought sweeping changes, drawing hundreds of people into the region, creating new communities, some which boomed and others which quickly faded. These years saw the transformation of the north, as the existing social fabric was shattered by the arrival of the construction crews and the developers who followed in their wake, and as a new social order emerged in its place.

The library shelves are filled with books about railway construction, and the sweeping changes that accompanied their seemingly unstoppable advance across the Canadian west. But in Eva MacLean's account of this period in the Hazelton region, we are introduced to a side of that era that has been rarely included in our understanding of the past. Her stories, delightfully told, give faces and personalities to the usually unknown men in the railway crews. She discusses her life and times, and vividly describes the community of the Hazelton area as it was transformed by the completion of the Grand Trunk Pacific. Eva MacLean has done more than just bring her own experiences to light; she has given a place in the historical record to the many men and few women who lived in this area during the construction boom.

Just who was Eva MacLean? As this book makes clear, she was a modest, unpretentious woman, highly regarded for her musical abilities and her community spirit. Raised in Ontario, she married Dan MacLean, a minister destined for a parish near Toronto. Shortly before their marriage, Eva learned that Dan had accepted a call to provide religious services to railway construction crews in northern British Columbia. To her parents' dismay — they were hoping that marriage to a minister would calm their rather high-strung daughter — they accepted the call and shortly thereafter headed west. They arrived in Old Hazelton, after a stop-over in Prince Rupert, in 1911 and remained there until 1915. Eva's first two children, Margaret and Marian, were born while in the area.

Dan MacLean was called to a church in Quesnel, where the couple's third child, Genevieve, was born, and then to Powell River. Their fourth child, Helen, was born almost immediately upon their arrival. The MacLeans continued to move around British Columbia: to a chicken farm in the Fraser Valley, to New Westminster, Burnaby, and Port Moody. Dan MacLean died in 1975 at the age of 95, leaving Eva alone after 64 years of marriage. Eva MacLean died in 1984, then 95 years old. Eva MacLean's life was very full, enriched by her family, and community and church activities. She was an accomplished singer and musician, helped her husband in his congregational work, wrote and published stories about her early experiences in British Columbia, and participated in a variety of community activities.

The stories in *The Far Land* are of an unusual sort, reflecting the author's character and her affinity for the people and the region. As a church organist, minister's wife, and mother, Eva MacLean brings an important perspective to bear on these crucial years. She was not part of the construction crews working on the railway, but she watched them work, and lived in their camps. As a woman in a largely male environment, she was very much aware of her minority status. In her account, Eva MacLean pokes fun at the pretensions of the social "elite" of the new railway towns, documents the toughness of the construction camps, illustrates the unique pressures and expectations placed on a "respectable" woman in a frontier setting, describes life among and with the First Nations, and recounts many different experiences and events in this rapidly changing region — a number of which are at odds with the standard version of Canada's "peaceable" frontier.

Eva MacLean was part of the great migrant work force that swept through northern British Columbia earlier this century, setting the North on a radically different path. She remained only a short time in the North and, even though it clearly left a permanent mark, did not often return. It is unfortunate that one finds such historical gems so infrequently, for we need to know so much more about the life and times of the people of northern British Columbia in the early 20th century. But the shortage of such memoirs makes the savouring of *The Far Land* that much sweeter.

Regions like northern British Columbia are often described as "new" and "developing," descriptions which ignore the generations-old histories of the First Nations and the earlier periods of non-Native settlement, railway construction, and resource development. We need, as we face the troubling and difficult task of determining a future for this part of British Columbia, to understand more fully the historical forces which shaped the North. *The Far Land* illuminates a part of northern British Columbia's past that has remained in the dark for too long. These captivating stories give a character and vitality to a society that very often peers out at us, undescribed and unknown, from sepia-toned photographs. Eva MacLean has done the North a great service by breathing life into these images from the past, and by providing such an authentic and compelling portrait of northern British Columbia in the days of the first railway boom.

Ken Coates
Author of *North to Alaska! 50 Years on the World's Most Remarkable Highway* and *Best Left as Indans: Native and White Relations in the Yukon Territory*
Prince George, British Columbia
1993

Introduction

THIS BOOK CONTAINS HUMAN INTEREST stories of the people who lived and the events that occurred there in the valleys of the Skeena and Bulkley Rivers during the construction of the Coast Division of the Grand Trunk Pacific Railway between 1911 and 1915. The stories are authentic, as history should be, and told as they were recorded in diaries, and from our personal experiences. Only a few of the characters have been given fictitious names, and all the principal characters are named authentically.

The locale may seem somewhat restricted, but the people were as cosmopolitan as those of most places in North America.

The prospectors were, for the greater number, Americans, Scots, Welsh, and a few Canadians from the Maritimes and Eastern Canada. The majority of the trappers were French-Canadians and Natives; the traders came there from many places, and the government employees were all English.

The men who built the railway came almost entirely from South Eastern Europe and Scandinavia, while the office workers were either Scots or Americans.

In these pages you will find stories of a famous Norse, of a former champion middle-weight's tragic death, and of a splendid pioneer from the mountains of Tennessee. There are many others who came to help build a country from the wilderness. You will also find the story of the two bank robberies in New Hazelton, told for the first time exactly as they happened.

I offer this book as a small contribution to Canadian history.

— Eva MacLean

CHAPTER ONE

From the
Sault
to the
Far Land

It was midnight and the sternwheel riverboat *Hazelton* was securely moored at the wooden wharf by the river's edge. Until now, the Skeena River meant nothing to me but a wavy black line across the northern end of the map of British Columbia, between the Rockies and the Pacific Ocean, some three thousand miles from all that was familiar.

It was my first night on board, and I was lying in a comfortable berth with the cool evening breeze fanning the air from the porthole.

I should have been asleep, for it had been a long and exciting day, and now the night was still. There was no sound of splashing or creaking from the paddle wheel, the engine was silent, and the only sound to be heard was the gentle slapping of the water against the side of the riverboat as the stream passed by on its tempestuous way to the sea. I was still awake and my mind was whirling with thoughts of my future in a strange country.

I knew nothing whatever about the place to which I was going, except that I would be living in a tent, a new experience for me. The people who lived there might present some problems, and this troubled me. When they heard of my destination, the reaction of those I had known at home in Ontario had not been reassuring. Some of them had been reading the new books about the Yukon written by Robert Service and Rex Beach, and they seemed to have the impression that it was a land of prospectors and miners, trappers, Natives and Mounties, gunmen, and prostitutes. "And," they asked, "would it be any different in Northern British Columbia, since it borders on the Yukon?"

Then I remembered the words of the dean as he addressed a graduating class several years before. He spoke directly to the class, and said, "Remember, you will be learning all your lives. You will be in life's school and you must hear, see, and try to understand what it means. Examine all theories thoroughly and think about them carefully. You are the coming generation and we look to you for leadership in this changing world."

I wondered if the lessons learned in my childhood and young womanhood would help me to understand this new life ahead. Since the future was unknown, I gave myself up to the memory of the time before I walked across the gangplank on my way to the new land.

My home was a farm not far from the St. Mary's River which flows out of Lake Superior. It was a beautiful countryside and cool breezes from that vast expanse of water swept down and drove away the heat of summer from the evening hours.

My father was a native of Cornwall, England, and came to Canada with his parents when he was a boy of ten. My mother was born in Toronto when that city was known as Muddy York, of parents from Northern Ireland. Her father had been a soldier in India in the army of Havelock's Highlanders, and had come to Canada when his term of service ended. Both families settled in Bruce County, and my parents met and married there. Before I was born, the youngest of nine children, my father moved to the newer part of the province in the Lake Superior country, and bought a farm which was then completely forested land. The family lived in a log cabin nearby while he and the three oldest sons cleared a section of the land, and with cedar and spruce trees built a log home for his family. Mother used to tell me proudly how he had hewed the logs with his broadaxe, and then with hammer, saw, and axe, he and the boys laid the foundation and built the house.

One of the nicest things about our childhood was that whatever one of our parents did, it was right with the other. It gave us a feeling of security and an atmosphere of love, loyalty, and kindness. Their first duty was to wrest enough from the trees and the land to give us food, clothing, and a modest education. Our lives were not as complex as some are today, and they did their best to bring us up to respect the basic virtues of honesty, kindness, and cleanliness. As a result, we all had strong bodies and some of their pioneer spirit.

At first, we had a team of oxen which I can only dimly remember, but when the heavy clearing was done and there were fields to be cultivated, they had to be discarded in favour of horses.

One of the great thrills of my childhood was the evening I was called to the window to see my father coming into the lane. I looked, and was speechless with excitement. Tied to the back of the ox drawn sleigh were two year-old colts. All I knew of horses was from pictures and an occasional glimpse of the neighbours' teams passing by, but I had dreamed of the day when we would have some of those beautiful animals.

Father lifted me up and moved close to the nearest colt, a dark bay with a white spot in his forehead. I threw my arms about his neck and then and there claimed him for my own. Both animals were ordinary unpedigreed horses, and while I have known many finer horses since, none has had a higher place in my affections than this colt, which I named Dick.

School days came, happy days mostly, even in winter when the snow was piled in drifts so high we had to use snowshoes. One of the highlights of those days was Friday afternoon, when from three to four o'clock we were allowed to have a programme of class singing, solos, and recitations. Sometimes our parents would come to hear us, and on one occasion I wished heartily they had stayed at home.

In our home, music was always with us. My father was a good musician with a bass-baritone voice we all loved to hear, and he taught every child in the family to read music and sing. One thing he abhorred was the newest form of music called ragtime. To him, the songs were inferior music with disgusting lyrics. One Friday, I had a new song for the class which I had found wrapped inside a parcel of school supplies. It was a song called "I Want My Lulu." The words being more or less meaningless to me, I didn't see any harm in it. Half way through the first verse, the door opened and my father and mother walked in. I almost stopped in the middle of a word, but the class seemed to be enjoying the song, so I finished it and went to my seat. I had a feeling that my father would be having a talk with me later. I wasn't disappointed, because although he did not mention it for a while, when I was going to bed that night and said goodnight to him, he looked at me sternly and said, "Never let me hear you sing a song like that one again." I really hadn't meant him to hear it that time.

Since I am an October child, I can never forget the autumn in Ontario. It is the heart of Indian summer, the time of rich harvest and rest from summer heat. It is the smell of burning leaves and stump piles, the blaze of scarlet and orange and bronze which covers the hillsides and the valleys like a flame, and makes your heart ache with the beauty until the maples, oaks, and poplars give their leaves back again to the breast of Mother Earth.

I remember the gardens with their abundance of orange carrots, red beets, green hubbard squash and cucumbers, the lighter shades of cabbages and cauliflower, and the pure gold of corn and pumpkins. Memories of the aroma of damp earth and the cool, sweet air are indelibly stamped on my mind.

In the orchards, the branches were bowed with ripening fruit, and the shelves of the storeroom were laden with rows of canned fruit, jellies, pickles, and jam. The field crops required every moment of daylight, and darkness fell before the barn chores were done. As pasture became scarce, the stock had to be fed in the barn, and the lamps were lighted long before we were called in to supper.

Lamps! When I think of trimming the wicks, filling the bowls and cleaning the chimneys of those coal-oil lamps, I give thanks for electricity. Still, when they shed their soft light on the supper table, they were somehow comforting and gave us a feeling of warmth and security.

Many farm homes in Ontario were like ours, a log house fashioned for warmth in winter and cool in summer, and as sturdy as the hearts of the men who built them. Our log home was a very comfortable place, and we slept on feather beds and laid our heads on pillows of softest goose down.

The greatest thrill of autumn was the annual agricultural fair which was held early in October. It lasted only three days, but the preparation took several weeks. A cyclone of activity took possession of the farms during the last few days before the fair as vegetables were selected and prepared, butter bricks decorated and set in the milk house to cool. The best hen and rooster pair, one or more calves, a gander and a pair of geese, were all chosen for the big show. Our brood sow Matilda was scrubbed with soap and water, not only to clean her skin but to obliterate some of that peculiar odour which pigs always seem to exude.She was the meanest animal on the farm, but she and her litter of piglets won several blue ribbons.

By the first day of the fair all entries had to be in their places, as most of the indoor judging was done that day. This cleared the decks for the second day when all the local dignitaries and their families gathered to see and be seen.

My most lasting impression of the fair was one of smells: hot buttered popcorn, fresh roasted peanuts, vegetables, fresh bread, and many flowers. The fumes of the mothballs in which fancy work had been packed since the year before, and many other odours, mingled with those of the barns beside the judging ring.

The butter in the dairy section was fascinating because it had been sculpted into many shapes and designs including portrayals of such politicians as Sir John A. MacDonald and Sir Wilfred Laurier. These resembled each other so closely one had to look at the cards beside them to tell them apart.

At eleven o'clock on the morning of the second day the citizens' band assembled on an upper balcony would burst into the strains of "The Maple Leaf Forever." Then out on the field in front of the grandstand, the town's mayor would declare the exhibition open. He was surrounded by members of the town council, officials of the agricultural society, and members of the Ontario Legislature and other politicians. Men in this last group were being very democratic, hail-fellow-well-met, and slap-on-the-backish, always mindful of the farmer's vote. At dinner that evening among groups of their city friends, they would probably refer to the rural population as hayseeds.

It was, however, a happy time for the farm children because for those three days we were the aristocracy, since some of our fathers were fair officials with badges, and it was from our farms that 90 percent of the exhibits came.

Halloween was the next celebration, and this occasion was observed in true country style, at parties where we dove for apples. Black cats and witches abounded, footballs made of rags soaked in kerosene were set alight and blazed as they flew through the air. Gates disappeared, wagons perched on top of barns, and outhouses were scattered over the landscape.

Then the hunting season opened and the guns came down off the wall: shotguns for birds, rifles for deer and moose. Each evening, the boys melted lead and molded bullets as they waited for snow to make tracking easy.

When they left for the hunting shanties on the high ground north of the farm lands, the folks at home waited anxiously for their return. Deer and moose were plentiful and a welcome addition to the larder.

Winter came on swift wings and we would wake up one morning to find our glorious autumn gone. I often thought of Bliss Carman's "Vagabond Song" and would repeat softly to myself,

> There is something in the autumn that is native to my blood,
> Touch of manner, hint of mood,
> And my heart is like a rhyme with the yellow and the purple
> And the crimson, keeping time . . .

It gave me a strange, yearning feeling that I wanted to go to some far place where there were hills of flame, high mountains and deep valleys and hear the call of "each vagabond by name." And here I was, in such a place in the northland of British Columbia.

When the Ontario winter came, it brought with it the sound of sleighbells, snowballs, tobogganing and skating and, best of all, Christmases! The simple pleasures and the inexpensive gifts of those days brought as much delight as the avalanche of costly gifts that are today's rule. As for Santa Claus, we were quite realistic about the old chap, knowing well that he was the Sunday School superintendent dressed up, but we loved him just the same.

The rest of the winter was cold and stormy, and there were some especially unpleasant aspects in the primitive way of life. Our water came from a well, and had to be pumped by hand for the stock as well as for the house. Sometimes the iron pump handle would be so cold it would stick to our warm hands and we occasionally lost bits of skin in separating them. And nobody who lived in the country in those days can forget the outdoor toilets, the dark, snow-edged paths to their doors, and the Eaton catalogues with snow between the pages! I shiver as I write. But soon it was spring again with the first cry of "sap's running." I can still taste the wonderful flavour of maple syrup on hotcakes, and the smooth and creamy maple sugar cakes.

Summer brought the busiest time of the year in a farming community, and the haying and harvesting left little time for anyone to rest. There were a few picnics, football games, and evening strolls, but picking wild raspberries and strawberries could hardly be called recreation. Blueberrying was another matter. It was like a picnic as a whole wagonload of young people would pile their lunches and their berry buckets into one big hayrack and drive off to a day on the jackpine flats by a small lake several miles up the river. Known as Mary Anne's Lake in my youth, it is now the site of a recently built modern airport. I was filled with regret when I heard of this, because the lake was named in honour of my mother, and she, too, is gone.

Summer ended the cycle of seasons and once again it was autumn.

In northern British Columbia, the sun rises very early on May days, and there was daylight by 2:30 in the morning. I was still unable to sleep and began to wonder if the people here would be very much different from those I had left behind in Ontario. They, too, were pioneers, but between East and West I had already found some contrasts. The natural candour and lack of pretence in those whom I had met since arriving in British Columbia was startling at first, but quite refreshing.

One could search for a long time and not find a more truly religious group than the farm people among whom I grew up. Religion was so deeply rooted in them that the church and its activities filled most of their spare time. Social life was almost entirely connected with the church and kindred organizations.

In my early years, the services were held in the schoolhouse, but later a church was built to provide a more suitable place to worship. The younger people wanted an organ and the church board felt they should have their way, so money was raised by various methods until they were able to buy one. The only person available to play it at that time was the minister, who was a very capable musician. A new hymnbook had recently been printed, but many of the tunes were not well known to the congregation.

We had always had a precentor to lead the singing. William Stephen, who came from Aberdeen, Scotland, had been brought up in the "Auld Licht" faith and was firmly opposed to the use of an organ. He said it was but a "kist o' whustles" and an "instrument o' the de'il," and that no good Presbyterian could sing "they Methody tunes." For many weeks he stood silent in the church he would not forsake even with an organ in it, while the rest of the congregation sang without a leader.

When the time came for the young minister to return to college, I became organist, at the age of fourteen. Now the precentor was in sore trouble as my father was not only his closest friend, but also the presiding elder. On the way to church that day, my father said, "play some of the old tunes, it'll be easier for him. Something everyone knows."

I was greatly relieved when it was announced that the first hymn would be Psalm 23, "The Lord is my Shepherd," a great favourite with everyone. Since I had learned to read music with the *Scottish Psalter* as my textbook, I knew I must play the melody of "wests," to which Mr. Stephen always sang that psalm. I saw our precentor's head raised quickly. He was the first person on his feet when the congregation rose, and his lovely voice was heard once more as he sang all the sadness out of his heart.

During the years I played the organ in that church his clear tenor voice and my father's great rolling bass, together with the voices of the congregation singing with pioneer fervour, made a sound of beauty which I have never forgotten.

Although these people were deeply religious, they seemed, oddly enough, narrow in their outlook on life. They were overready to condemn "sinners" who had transgressed the church's moral code. There was also a great deal of racial prejudice, perhaps more than there is today. They would not deliberately harm the people of another race, but they considered them inferior Anglo-Saxons. They were all foreigners! Even the French, who had been Canadians as long as the English, and the aboriginal people who had been here long before, and were the only true Canadians, were so considered. They called the Natives "savages," which I thought peculiar, because I knew that many members of Canada's "first families" boasted of Native blood in their veins.

The tribes nearest us along the St. Mary's River were Ojibwas and Chippewas, and all lived in poverty.

Seldom was any employment given them except the most menial jobs, and then they were paid less than white men doing the same work.

Our church's rules were strict: dancing and card playing were taboo; there was to be no secular reading or singing on Sunday.

The church fathers didn't realize that such senseless condemnation of anything beyond these rules was the greatest sin of all. Each denomination felt that the others were possibly Christians, but misguided. It was frustrating to me in spite of my happy childhood.

The year I turned sixteen the question of what I was to do with my life was my chief concern. Mother thought I should remain at home, continue my musical studies, and wait for some good man to ask me to marry him. Father was more realistic; he said I should be learning something which would enable me to earn my living in case the man was a long time arriving. I agreed with him, so Mother was overruled and I enrolled in a newly established business college. I was excited and pleased at the thought of earning my own living, especially as so few girls had entered the business world in those days.

One day shortly after the decision had been made, we had a caller, Mrs. Elmer Baxter, who lived on a farm nearby. She was an austere woman, much given to good works; the more unpleasant the duty, the more she enjoyed it. After the usual words of greeting she plunged into her subject.

"Tell me," she asked, "is it true that you are sending Eva to business college to be a stenographer?"

"Yes," my mother answered brightly, "Eva has always wanted to earn her own living and she is delighted to have the opportunity."

"My dear friend" — and here Mrs. Baxter lowered her voice to a mere whisper — "do you realize that she will be all alone in an office with *MEN?*"

Mother's voice had considerable ice in it as she quickly changed the subject. But she was troubled, I know, because she said to me later, "You know, Eva, you are pretty young to be going away from home. You must be very careful in your behaviour at all times, because people like Mrs. Baxter require little provocation to make things rough for a girl."

I didn't answer for a moment because I was remembering the pale, unwholesome face of the Baxter boy. He and a few of his friends used to make life miserable for the girls in the elementary school. Then I said, "Don't worry, mother, and don't forget that I went to school with the son of that old busybody, and if that isn't training in how to take care of yourself, I don't know what would be."

I attended business college for several months, and, after graduating as a full-fledged secretary, found my first job with an American lumber company. The work was light and pleasant though some of the business transactions worried me slightly, as I had been taught that honesty was one of the basic virtues. At least the lumber was sweet smelling! But where, oh where was the romance which was supposed to come into my life?

After a year or two I was able to get work in the offices of a large city corporation, a much-prized job as the company had instituted an ascending wage schedule at a time when financial and economic factors were as important as they are now.

During the years I spent among typewriters, pencils, notebooks and ledgers, I discovered a few things which I did not mention to anyone because I feared I might be wrong. To differ from others in such matters as religion, social attitudes, and what constituted education meant *someone* was mistaken. I was confused and not a little worried about my newly obtained knowledge, for I had come into contact with racial discrimination, hypocrisy, class distinctions, and other ideas which robbed me of many illusions.

As for finding the "right" man, after one or two teenage romances, I decided to marry nobody but a professor of music who could help me with my musical career.

A restlessness enveloped me, greatly encouraged by letters from my brother Tom, who had gone to Alberta some years before and had written glowing accounts of the life in that province. When he suggested that I travel to Alberta to see it for myself, I resigned from my job and left for a vacation to discover if it was as interesting as he claimed.

It was there, in that perfect setting of moonlight on the prairie and surrounded by dashing — and some not so dashing— cowboys, that I met the man who made me forget the professor of music who had been my earlier romantic objective.

My parents were not enthusiastic about having me go so far from home, but my longing for new experiences and new faces was too strong to be denied. Life in city offices, so different from my childhood on the farm, had made me uncertain of myself and reminded me of the advice offered to students by the dean of the business college.

"Find out for yourselves what makes the world go round," he said, "and do not accept any theories which your own intelligence rejects without careful study . . . ."

I knew I wanted to get away from everything I had known so that I could acquire new knowledge and experience; perhaps, too, I would learn what made me so rebellious about many of the things I had been taught. My youthful enthusiasm for travel — to see more of the world — played a part too, and in those days, Alberta seemed to be the on other side of the world from Ontario.

Tom was farm foreman on the Lazy-JW Ranch, which was owned by Charlie Williamson, locally known as the Old-Timer because he was a veteran of the 1885 North-west Rebellion. He and Mrs. Williamson added their invitation to Tom's and I went directly to their home on my arrival in Alberta. The ranch was on the banks of the Little Bow River at the old Blackfoot Crossing, a place well known to early settlers.

This wide prairie land was indeed a new experience and one which I have never forgotten. It was on the first day there that I met Tom's friend, Donald MacLean, whose ancestors had emigrated to Nova Scotia many years before, from Mull, an island in the Hebrides, off the west coast of Scotland.

Donald, whom I called Dan, was a graduate of Pictou Academy and Dalhousie University; he had completed two years in Pine Hill Theological College, and, after much study and practice in the diseases of animals, he had received a degree in veterinary medicine from the Ontario Veterinary College. He was now a student at Knox College in Toronto. While Dan spent his vacation on the prairie, he preached on Sundays; on week days he broke wild horses to the saddle, and he doctored sick animals all over the district. How he found time to fall in love, I don't know, but in less than a month we were engaged to be married.

The rancher had provided a mare named Buttons for me, and so Dan, on his own horse Silvertip, and I rode for many hours across the prairie. I was intrigued by the gun swung low on Dan's belt, but Tom whispered a warning not to mention it to our parents as they were not accustomed to preachers who wore sidearms.

Dan and Tom explained that guns were a necessity when men worked with horses and cattle on the open range, when firearms could be used to stop a stampede, prevent an accident, shoot gophers, or to shoot a steer for meat during a roundup. I learned that there were other uses for guns, even for a preacher.

One day when the three of us were riding across a range owned by a character called Old Tom Purcell, Dan told me the story of the man who was alleged to have started with only a good rope and a horse, down in Montana. He left that state shortly after his wife had been found dead at the bottom of a cliff, tied to the saddle of a mule — at least so some people said. Now, he had acquired a wide spread of land in Alberta, stocked it with horses, built a good home and settled down. Even with all his prosperity, some hinted, he was adding the occasional colt or calf to his herds without the formality of a bill of sale.

One day a neighbouring rancher had come for Dan saying that one of his best colts had cut himself badly on a barbwire fence and was bleeding profusely.

Dan went with him to treat the colt's wound, a deep one requiring many stitches, but the animal soon recovered and was turned out with the rest of the herd.

Shortly afterwards he disappeared without a trace until a passing rider saw the colt in Old Tom's corral, and reported this to the police. One of the many Purcell Ranch riders learned of the report and told his employer, so when the police arrived there was no sign of the colt. The police made a thorough search of the ranch and found the colt at the bottom of an old covered well. Old Tom was arrested for horse stealing and lodged in Lethbridge jail. Dan's testimony and recognition of the scar proved the old man's guilt and he was sentenced to several years' imprisonment, although he was released from jail before the end of his term because of his advanced age. He returned to his ranch, and from there he sent a message to Dan that he was looking for him and would shoot him on sight. Dan's answer was a short one: "Don't miss, Tom, because I won't!"

I returned from my vacation in Alberta and began at once to look for the job I needed if I were to gather items for my trousseau. Dan and I were to be married in the following autumn after his graduation. At home, the emotions of my family were somewhat mixed. They were all glad I was to marry a minister, as ministers were in high repute in Ontario, and they thought my new husband might have a sobering effect on me. While they didn't exactly disapprove of me, I had broken a few family traditions, such as learning to dance, and they doubted my stability of character. Since they had met Dan on his way to Toronto, they liked him very much, and they wondered if he shouldn't have a more devout wife, or at least a more dignified one.

Nonetheless, all my female relatives began to sew, making quilts, sheets and pillow cases, embroidering towels and linens, and all the mountains of under-wear young women wore in the early part of the twentieth century. I knew my departure would leave them lonely, especially my father, as he would miss my music keenly. They were the kind of people who believed a young woman should marry and have children, however, so they gave their approval gladly.

Dan wrote that he had accepted a call to a church near Toronto, and that letter brought my possible future into sharper focus. One day I began reading over the marriage ceremony in my mother's prayer book: "I, Eva Estelle, take thee Donald Redmond . . . ."

My heart ached a little as the sense of religion instilled in me as a child had faded considerably. I was truly sorry for Dan, who would be marrying such an unreligious woman, as well as for myself. I wondered, too, whether I could tolerate life in a manse, or, on the other hand, if I could stand life without Dan, when I heard my brother calling me. "Eva, don't you know there's a letter for you?"

I ran into the house and opened the letter, reading it hastily. When I finished reading, there was such a strange look on my face that my family thought something awful had happened, and they asked, "Is anything wrong with Dan?"

"No, of course not," I stammered, "But here, I'll read it to you."

"Last night the Superintendent of Missions for British Columbia came to Knox and spoke to our class," he wrote. "He asked for volunteers to go on a mission in northern British Columbia, to a place called Hazelton on the Skeena River. None of the other fellows seemed anxious to go, but I couldn't get to him fast enough. Eve[1], we're going north to the Skeena Valley where I'll be a missionary to the men on construction of the new transcontinental railway they are building through to the coast. I hope you will forgive me for taking you so far away, but we'll have to go right after graduation. Can you be ready? I'll be up there several years and I won't go without you, so write . . . ."

Mother was shocked by this development, although she took it quietly. To her, British Columbia was almost a foreign land, but to me the idea of living in such a far-off place spelled adventure. Dan was going to be a minister, but the country would be exciting and new. Only the look on my mother's face kept me from shouting for joy; she was quietly weeping over a pan of biscuits she was taking from the oven. That, I think, was when I grew up, leaving a carefree girlhood behind to become an adult.

With only one month in which to prepare for the wedding, instead of the six months which had been planned, I said a silent farewell to at least half the

---

1   Eva was also known as Eve among her family and friends.

trousseau I would have had. I knew it was time to shake off my excitement and to prepare for this drastic change in plans.

On the Sunday before our wedding and our departure for western Canada, I attended church and played the organ there for the last time. I knew well what my friends had been thinking about our new destination, but there was much worse to come. When the elderly Scottish minister was in the middle of a long prayer, he suddenly became unctuous, and in pleading voice he prayed, "And now, O Lord, we earnestly beseech Thee to protect this young sister and brother who are leaving us to carry the gospel to that far land where sin doth abound and Satan lifteth up his head, that they may be kept unspotted from the world in that place that knows not God."

I was stunned by the audacity of his words, and as I looked around the church, I discovered that not one head was raised other than mine. The entire congregation agreed with him. How could he, a Christian minister, so smugly spread a blanket of condemnation over a country and its people, knowing nothing whatever of either! If the salvation of the "far land" depended upon the Church, then he should have discovered that missionaries of several denominations had been in that country for many years. If their services to the people had taught them no more than this man knew, they might just as well have stayed at home.

After living for six years in the business world of my home town, I didn't think I would have much trouble remaining unspotted anywhere in the world.

Time passed quickly and in May our wedding day arrived. Everyone said it was a beautiful wedding, and the look on my mother's face was the only shadow, as she listened to our vows. I had warned her not to cry and she was trying bravely, but she would have looked more cheerful if she had cried. My father stood just behind me with his head high and his face stern.

The farm gave up its choicest chickens, vegetables, and cream for our wedding luncheon, and for the beautiful basket which had been packed for us to take on the train. It was hard to realize I was going away until I saw the determined cheerfulness on the faces of the family and close friends. Then we were on our way to the railway station. Dan was most uncomfortable, as he

Eva and Dan on their wedding day April 19, 1922, at her family home in Sault Ste. Marie, Ontario.

suspected many of my friends would be there to see us off, probably well supplied with rice and confetti, and he couldn't face that. He said determinedly, "We aren't going all the way across the continent with rice in our hair and that's that!"

Bitterly disappointed and in something of a temper, I consented to his plan to cross the river on the ferry and board our train on the American side. I knew my friends would be disappointed, maybe angry, and I sulked for an hour. This was scarcely nice of me on our wedding day, but I soon recovered and forgave him.

Calm sobriety was the keynote of our journey, and so well did we succeed in our deception that the second day on the train a woman asked me if we had any family. I answered sadly, "No, not yet. It's a disappointment to us but we're still hoping."

Our first stop in Alberta was at Fort Macleod, the scene of many battles between cowboys, miners from the Crowsnest Pass, Natives, and Mounties. The old barracks of the Northwest Mounted Police still commanded a view of the entire surrounding country, although their headquarters had been moved to Regina. Fort Macleod is a historic town and was then one of the last of the "wild west" places on the prairies. From there we went directly to the Williamson ranch where we had first met, and there our welcome was heartwarming. And I was relieved to learn that Old Tom Purcell had died in bed without his boots or gun.

For two long sunny days we loafed about, talking to our friends and eating enormous meals. On the third day we went for a ride across the prairie on Buttons and Silvertip, returning home weary and happy. We retired early that night. At about 2:00 in the morning, the earth and sky exploded, or so I thought.

Guns were blazing, cowbells ringing, harrow discs banging, and blood-curdling yells from the throats of about fifty men split the silence of the night. I lay perfectly still, paralyzed with fear until Dan said, chuckling, "Just the boys giving us a bit of a welcome."

I was delighted that we were still alive and uninjured, as I didn't think so much noise was possible on earth. Dan went to the window where an early edition of Matt Dillon was perched on a ladder just outside with a six-shooter in one hand and a cowbell in the other, both in continuous action. Dan said quietly, "How about cooling down now, we're awake." As if we could possibly be anything else! Our host, the Old-Timer, came to the foot of the stairway and called, "Better get dressed and come down; they won't stop until you do."

We donned our clothes in record time and dashed down the stairs and out to the ranch kitchen where we found the long table spread with a bountiful supper. The room was filled with ranchers and their wives, as well as the single young riders who had gathered from as far away as fifty miles to greet us. When my fright had subsided sufficiently to allow me to speak naturally, I began to enjoy myself. The party lasted until dawn, and weary beyond description, we went back to bed and slept until noon.

After this reception I was sure nothing could surprise me, but many things delighted me. For the rest of the week we watched the herds being brought in for the spring roundup. The Williamson's daughter Carrie brought in a herd of mares and colts, and swam them across the Blackfoot Crossing of the Little Bow River into the corral. To my amazement, even the youngest colt knew enough to stay on the upstream side of its mother so the current could not carry it away.

The next morning, Dan was asked if he would like to ride one of the green broncos which had to be saddlewise when it was sold. He was delighted, and I thought it would be fun to watch as I had never seen him riding an unbroken horse. It was, at first, as I watched him rope and blindfold the one he was to ride.

Dan landed in the saddle and ripped off the blindfold. Immediately the horse was transformed into a whirlwind of fury, bucking, twisting, and squealing with rage. I closed my eyes and put both hands over my face. The boys were shouting encouragement as Dan slapped the ears of his horse with his folded sombrero, to persuade the animal to get all the frustration out of his system as quickly as possible. Then, after what seemed to me a long time, I heard someone say, "That was a dandy ride, Dan; college hasn't spoiled you a bit. "

I could see Dan still in the saddle while the horse stood trembling by the corral fence. When he asked me how I liked it, I said quickly, "Oh, it was just wonderful!"

"How do you know, you didn't see it."

"Well, I promise to watch next time. After all, we are on our honeymoon and I had visions of you being picked up in a basket, because that horse looked like a wild thing to me."

I climbed down off the corral fence and started to cross the open space to the gate when I came face to face with a calico bronco standing about six feet from me. He snorted wildly, eyes bulging and nostrils flared. I just rose up like a helicopter and sailed over that fence amid roars of laughter from the men gathered around. After that, I stayed out of the corral.

We spent a few more days at the ranch and I learned to appreciate the beauty of the prairie, of the wide expanse of fields and the tremendous bowl of the sky, infinitely larger than the sky I was accustomed to seeing, reaching down to the horizon at eye level.

Some parts of southern Alberta were still open range, but that was fast disappearing as a surge of homesteaders had been pouring in ever since the land had been thrown open for settlement. Some of the homesteaders were farmers from the eastern provinces, while others were settling on the land for the first time, but it was difficult for either group to adjust to prairie conditions. The tough bunch grass of that virgin soil could not be turned over as easily as the well-cultivated ground of the older provinces, and it required four horses to plough even a small area each day.

For the ranchers who had been running their herds on open range, it was heartbreaking to go riding across the prairie in the evening and find themselves blindly colliding with barbwire strung around a newly claimed homestead.

Horses suffered many serious injuries, as they were sensitive to pain and fought the wire in panic, while cows would back away slowly and escape uninjured. It was necessary for those who staked homesteads to string at least one strand of wire around it as quickly as possible to make sure of their claims. Wire was expensive, and the posts had to be hauled from the foothills, fifty miles to the west.

The result was, naturally, friction between the ranchers and the homesteaders. Each cursed the other soundly, but to no avail. The farmers were there to stay and the ranchers were forced to adjust themselves to the new conditions. Through hard times and arduous toil the farmers survived and wheat began to cover the wide lands. The ranchers either trimmed their herds to suit the smaller pastures, or moved them to the foothill country. Some even began to plant grain.

The land seemed lonely to me, bereft of trees and hills, and the green grass of my native Ontario, but in spite of all that I had to admit there was something thrilling in the tremendous space, the glorious sunshine, and the sunsets which were breathtaking in their beauty.

Our holiday was nearly over and soon we were on our way westward through the Rockies, over the Cascades and the Coast Range to the Pacific coast and

Vancouver. From the day we arrived in that beautiful city, my heart went out to it, and, ever since, any part of British Columbia is home to me.

We stayed in Vancouver for a week, visiting friends, shopping, and sightseeing. The natural grandeur of Stanley Park with its thousands of immense trees standing straight and tall, the flowers, and the blue water surrounding it, made it seem like another world.

When we were shopping for furniture for our new home, we didn't dream that we would be living in a tent with space for nothing other than the absolute essentials: a stove, a table and chairs, and a bed. Dan bought a large oak desk for his books, and a kitchen cabinet for me. When we went to the store's kitchenware department we found ourselves buying, almost surreptitiously, a fish slice, before looking at pots and pans.

The trip up the coast on the steamer *Prince George* was an unforgettable experience. The weather was clear and bright, warmer than the Mays we had known, while the light breeze filled our lungs with the delicious sea air.

The ship glided on water as smooth as glass through the Inside Passage between the islands and the mainland. We seemed to be sailing on a lake which had a continually changing shore line of snow-capped mountains, valleys, and tall green trees, always beautiful.

One of the ship's officers was a Norwegian who told us that even the shores of his land were not more beautiful than these, at which we gazed in speechless wonder.

We arrived in Prince Rupert to find a town in the process of being born. Some of the streets were planks on top of muskeg, while others were being blasted out of solid rock. One man had blasted the mountainside into sheer walls for two sides of his tennis court. Trees made the third wall, and his house was the fourth. All types of buildings were under construction, from the handsome clubhouse on the hill to the hotel by the water front. There were small shacks side by side with large new houses, tents, and modest business blocks.

The people were a miscellaneous group, businessmen and their families, real estate dealers, land developers, construction men, and workers of all kinds —

each hoping to make a fortune somehow in this new country soon to be connected with the rest of Canada by the building of the Grand Trunk Pacific Railway.

The atmosphere was charged with light-hearted optimism and faith in the new world of endeavour, while the exhilarating sea air swept across the harbour. It was infectious and we thanked the fates which had sent us there to share in the building of this great gateway to the Pacific.

I found the struggle for social supremacy among a few of the women rather amusing. The wives of the railway and construction company officials, and of those who had made substantial fortunes in real estate and other enterprises, were determined to found a caste of society to offset the more democratic ways of their menfolk.

The wife of a company official with whom I was having tea one afternoon, was asked by her husband to give a tea or luncheon for the bride of one of his associates. She exploded, "Give a luncheon for her! Why, she was my maid only a year ago before she went to the hotel as a waitress. Why should I entertain her?"

Her husband seemed amused and answered dryly, "And what were you doing when I met you in Colorado twenty years ago?"

She opened her mouth to answer, but no words came. Then she turned away with flushed face, muttering, "All right. I'll give her a luncheon."

She had been a chambermaid in the hotel in which her husband had lived while he was working on a construction job in that city. Those with pretensions to being members of high society had a problem as it was impossible to say who came from which side of the tracks, since the tracks were all but obliterated in the new town. These women were foolish to consider such things, as everyone had the same reason for coming to the new country: to help build it and make a living in jobs that were equally honest and admirable.

Dan and I found them kind, generous, and friendly people; and I was unsuccessful in my search for the signs of abounding sin, or the Old Boy lifting up his head. Everyone was too busy to get into much trouble with the law, and the law was just as busy trying to get rich as the people were.

It may easily have been that the farther I travelled from Eastern Canada, the more at home I felt. In spite of my happy and secluded childhood, I seemed to have been born again in these strange surroundings. I was experiencing one of those lessons the dean had mentioned, and I hoped to profit from it.

Our first taste of grilled salmon, fresh from the salt water, was one of the highlights of our stay in Prince Rupert, and laid to rest forever the bogey of having to eat salmon as a main dish. However, we ate more salmon that week than we were to see in a year in the northern valley of the Skeena where the river was supposed to be teeming with the big, red fish.

Sunday came and with it Dan's ordination and induction into the church. Several members of the Session of the Vancouver church came with us to officiate in the ceremony, and by eleven o'clock we were all assembled in the barnlike theatre where the ordination was to take place. Just as the ceremony was about to begin, it was noticed that the stage floor was dirty and splintered, which would be disastrous to the assembled ministers' black robes. One of the local elders sent his son home for some cushions to kneel on during the service. The house was some distance away and the boy returned just in time to drop the cushions on stage and depart hastily.

As the moderator looked with satisfaction on the cushions, his eyes widened in horror. The one in front of him pictured a barroom scene with bottles of whiskey conspicuously displaying the brand name. The one in front of Dan showed an almost nude figure of a woman holding aloft in one hand a glass which appeared to contain whiskey, while in the other hand was a pack of cards. Both pictures were painted on in brilliant colours.

As the other men glanced downward it was evident their faces wore suppressed grins and their voices trembled with an emotion not wholly sacred. Dan looked quite devout as he knelt for their blessing. He said he didn't dare open his eyes lest he roar with laughter at the doubtful foundation he had when he received his "Reverend."

That evening we were guests at dinner in the home of the elder whose son had brought the cushions, and with much laughter, the matter was explained.

When Jackie reached home he found the door locked, so he ran into the cabin of a prospector who lived next door. He picked up the cushions from the homemade armchairs and ran back to the theatre. The elder had to undergo some ribbing before he proved they were not his. One of the other guests was a classmate of Dan's from Dalhousie University. He was a Prince Edward Islander who had graduated from Pine Hill College but had never taken a pastorate. He was in business in Prince Rupert, and when asked why he had left the church, he told us, "I couldna preach. I was too shy and my Highland tongue chist made them laugh. I could tell you a story about my last tryout for a church . . . "

"Come on, Hector, tell them," urged Dan, who had heard the story before.

"Well, it was a country congregation up in New Brunswick and there was many young men and they loved the fetching. They only come to church to see what fun they could have and made so much noise, I couldna stand it." A slow grin spread over Hector's face as he recalled the incident. "When I was startin' my sermon one of them called out, 'Can ye heal the sick or raise the dead, preacher?' and they all laughed. "I looked him straight in the eye as I pondered what to do." (Hector was six feet two inches in height, weighed about two hundred and thirty pounds of solid flesh and muscle. He had worked in a logging camp to pay his way through college, and was still in excellent condition.)

"Then I said, 'Na, I canna heal the sick or raise the dead, but there is one thing I can do, py cheorge, I can cast out the teffels.'

"I laid down the Book and walked down the aisle to that young man and I lifted him over my head and threw him right outside through an open window. Then I came back and finished the service." He added simply, "I haf preached no more since that day."

By the time the laughter had subsided, we knew it was necessary for us to say goodnight to our host, as Dan had to be on his way upriver by sunrise. I was to stay in Prince Rupert until he had time to pitch a tent for us to live in, as the overcrowded condition of Hazelton made a tent a necessity. I was much disappointed, but since he was travelling on one of the Foley, Welch and Stewart freight carriers, there was no accommodation for a woman. I would have to wait another week.

CHAPTER TWO

Up the Skeena by Riverboat

Northern British Columbia is a land of colour and romance, sometimes cold and cruel, but with a hypnotic charm for those who have lived there. The splendour of those green valleys cradling turbulent rivers; the hills so thickly wooded with giant trees; the towering mountains with their snow-capped peaks reaching into the clear blue sky; the pure air and the brilliant sunlight and moonlight; and the immensity of the country as a whole, which may be a little frightening. One may hate or love it, but either way, it is unforgettable.

Early in the morning of May 25, 1911, I stood on the wharf in Prince Rupert, trembling with excitement, watching my trunks and personal belongings being carried aboard the riverboat *Hazelton,* which was to be my home for nearly a week. Our furniture would not be on this boat as there wasn't sufficient space for it, but I was going anyway. I was supposed to wait until Dan sent for me, but in spite of the kindness of new-found friends, I was determined to travel up the Skeena by this sailing. My Prince Rupert friends escorted me across the gangplank and committed me to the care of the entire crew and passenger list. They were urged to deliver me safely to my husband, now nearly two hundred miles away. I was the only woman aboard, and I couldn't help wondering what

Riverboat Port Simpson at Hazelton wharf. A sister boat to the Hazelton that carried Eve up the Skeena from Prince Rupert. Rocher de Boule Mountain in the background.

Mrs. Baxter would say if she knew I was going to be alone with *M-E-N* for nearly a week!

The prospect embarrassed me, but only because I didn't know much about those old sourdoughs who were to be my companions. The care and attention they showered on me showed women were scarce in that part of the country, and they were, therefore, to be cherished. I wasn't allowed to feel lonely for a minute. They talked to me, brought me cups of tea as well as candy, and magazines which I did not read as there was no opportunity. It was almost as though they were afraid I would change my mind and swim back to Prince Rupert. They need not have worried because I could not have been induced to go back.

The skipper was Captain Gardiner, whose navigational skills were much needed on that narrow and winding river. The mate's name was McKenzie, an obliging and efficient young man. There were two engineers, several deckhands, and cabin boys who doubled as waiters at mealtimes, a Chinese cook and his helper.

The passengers were mostly miners and prospectors returning to their claims after a winter holiday in the south. There was a doctor on his way home to the Bulkley Valley town of Aldermere; a mining engineer on his way to supervise his father's copper mines on Rocher de Boule mountain; the chief engineer for Foley, Welch and Stewart; the contractors who were building the railway from Edmonton west to the coast. There were a couple of salesmen, or agents, and one woman — myself.

The riverboat itself was a lovely thing, clean and shining, with neat staterooms, comfortable berths with snowy linen. The food was excellent and our appetites were enormous. I felt my spirits rising with every mile of that wonderful journey.

The birth and heritage of the vessel's cabin boys puzzled me, for, whether they were wearing their dark outfits or waiters' white coats, they looked somewhat like Native youths — but not quite. Sometimes I was sure they were Japanese, and one day I asked the captain which nationality they were. He smiled as he answered a bit dryly, "Both! Here on the coast there has been considerable intermingling of the two races, and I must say they are very smart boys, and good workers. I don't wonder you were puzzled, and in fact they look so much alike that sometimes I get mixed up myself, which makes the boys laugh."

"They certainly take great care of the passengers, and they are very polite and obliging. In fact, there are ocean steamers with much less efficient and polite staff," I told him. "I must thank them before we reach our destination. Would it be all right to give them a tip?"

"Rather you didn't," he replied, "but I think you could give them some of that candy I understand you have been receiving."

And this I did, although it seemed small reward for the service I had received. Nothing but superlatives could describe that trip up the river. The old sternwheeler moved slowly along, the wheel turning steadily at a speed never exceeding three miles an hour against the current, tying up when it was too dark for the captain to see the channel clearly through the rapid waters. Since it was nearly midnight when real darkness descended and only three hours before the sun rose again, we were on our way long before I was awake in the morning.

I feasted my eyes on an ever-changing panorama of swift white water, green woods, and purple mountains with their dazzling white peaks. The meals were bountiful and I ate ravenously of the wide variety of fresh foods provided. The rest of the day was spent in listening to the happy chatter of the old-timers. As it grew dark that first night on the river, the *Hazelton* edged its way to a wooden wharf to tie up until daylight. We all went ashore and the men built a bonfire on the bank beside the river. It was good to stand on solid ground, but I was still fearful of the giant trees and the country in general. There was something ghostly about those trees with their trellised moss, delicate and dark green, that covered trunks and branches as high as one could see. The miners told me moss grew on trees only near the coast, encouraged by the damp climate, but that I would not see any moss further upriver.

When the boat reached Kitselas Canyon, the water was rising rapidly from the spring freshets, and the captain told us we would have to walk around the canyon to the other side, where another boat, the *Port Simpson*, was waiting to take us the rest of the way. As we approached the canyon I had heard the old-timers' stories of boats that had gone down there during the highwater season, and my teeth were chattering with fright. I was thankful when the captain announced that he would not attempt to go through.

We disembarked willingly and walked the mile of road which skirted the raging canyon, happy to get the much-needed exercise. The freight wagons passed us on their way with the freight and cargo, but when we arrived at the upper end of the canyon, my heart stood still. The men were transferring the freight from the wagons to the *Port Simpson*, and I saw my trunks and crates of personal belongings, with my precious wedding gifts of china and glassware, being rolled end over end down the plank into the bowels of the ship. Tears of rage filled my eyes, and I said a silent goodbye to the things we had packed with such care. But I wept too soon: our packing had been more careful than I knew, and nothing was broken. I had a strong suspicion, however, that when

27

the next boat came up the river, our furniture would arrive in splinters, because the crates in which it was packed were very flimsy. I was not mistaken that time.

We travelled on up the river, once in a while drawing in to shores bordered by what looked to me like the forest primeval, but obviously home to a crowd of settlers, both Native and white, who came to greet our arrival. While the crew unloaded the boxes of supplies, Natives piled wood on the deck to feed the engines' fires. Then, with a friendly waving of hands and tooting of the whistle, we moved out into the river current and were again on our way. I had decided by this time that travelling on a riverboat up the Skeena River, the big wheel turning steadily, sending cascades of water splashing from the paddles, and the steady chug-chug of the engine, was the most exciting thing I had ever experienced.

There was a variety of passengers on the trip. As the only female on board, particularly having come from the far side of the continent, and going into this country to make my home, I was the object of curiosity.

Among my fellow passengers was Mr. Van Arsdol, chief engineer in charge of the railway's coast division. A man in his young middle age, he spoke with a Texas accent and had an unusual appearance. He was tall, wore a long drooping mustache, a Windsor tie, and a large cream-coloured sombrero. His voice was soft, and he spoke so quietly that we had to listen intently to everything he was saying. The way we clustered around him, I sometimes wondered just what kind of story the crew might think he was telling us. Mr. Van Arsdol devoted himself to entertaining me; I listened to his all but inaudible voice until my ears were aching, but when I could hear him above the throbbing of the engines and the splash of the wheel, he was most interesting. One day he told me about the problems of building a railway grade through such mountainous country, which required much rock blasting, and the dangers created by sliding gumbo. I asked him, "What do you do with the young relatives of the directors who are sent out from the east to be given jobs?"

He looked startled. "What do you know about an engineer's job?" he asked.

"I was the secretary to the chief engineer of a railway under construction in northern Ontario," I explained, "and I'm really enjoying your talk about grades and slides and dangerous work. We had much the same situation."

He stared at me, seemingly surprised to find me intelligent enough to be secretary of a chief engineer. Then he smiled warmly through his astonishment and looked at me with interest.

"I'm so glad this talk of slides, gumbo and rock blasting hasn't bored you, Mrs. MacLean. I was afraid it might, but it seems to be the only subject I'm interested in right now."

"You haven't answered my question about relatives yet," I reminded him.

"Now I know you have worked for a chief engineer! Well, I look them over, and if they are a bit cocky from being spoiled at home, I put them in the woods as axemen. Sometimes they cut their foot the first week out and go back where they came from. Some make good and stay. My best foreman didn't know an axe from a pick when he first came out."

In the long summer evenings, we all sat out on deck and watched as the gallant little riverboat chugged its way up that winding, twisting river. The old-timers had the most gruesome tales of men who had fallen into the river and had never been seen again. One talkative old prospector told me, "We're pretty close to Hardscrabble, one of the worst riffles on the river. Many a poor fellow lost his life trying to round that point in a canoe, I can tell you."

I asked weakly, "Don't they ever get out of the river?"

"Not fer weeks," his eyes were twinkling with mischief. "Then their bodies turn up here at Floater's Flats, which we're passing right now." If he wished to frighten me he certainly had succeeded.

I went to bed with the coldest feeling in my feet. I didn't stay awake long, however, because I was asleep when the first crash came. I was out of my berth in a second and looking out of the porthole I saw several of the crew and passengers clustered around just outside my cabin, all talking at once. The boat had shuddered, swung sideways, crashing into the rock wall on the opposite side and it was slipping back down river. I had visions of my body being fished out of Floater's Flats sometime next year, but a crew member told me not to worry; nothing serious had happened, he reassured me.

If that was nothing at all, I hoped most sincerely that "something" wouldn't happen. I crept back into my bed as the engines came to life once more to try again the riffle which had thrown it out of the channel. I snuggled down into the blankets and tried to go to sleep. Then, another crash! Another sickening shudder and backward slide.

This time I found my voice and demanded to know just what was going on. Mr. Van Arsdol's quiet voice came from the darkness of the deck.

"There's no danger, Mrs. MacLean, it was just the guard rail was broken when the boat swung over against the rocks. Everything is under control, so don't be alarmed." (Just for the record that guard rail was a piece of twelve by twelve timber!)

"Yeah," came the voice of the teller of disaster stories, "ye can go right back to sleep, 'cause the captain's goin' to tie up right here and wait till sunup."

By the time the sun was high in the sky again, we were long past the dangerous riffle that had filled my dreams with terror. We were told that the steering gear had been changed shortly before this trip, and the captain wasn't accustomed to power steering and had turned the wheel too far on the riffle, so the current had swung the boat sideways.

About noon we came to Minstgonish, a Native village where many large totems lined the shore. I wanted to land and examine them more closely but I was unable to find anyone to accompany me.

This was puzzling because everyone had been so kind and this was the first favour I had asked. The explanation was not long coming. "Ye see, lady, there's a missionary that runs this village and he don't allow no smokin' or drinkin' or even a little cuss-word on shore, so we stays on the boat. We call that place 'Heaven,' and I don't reckon any of us could stand the strain." After four days on the boat with these kindly, humorous but fluently profane old sourdoughs, I could see what he meant.

One young man, whose father owned copper mines in the district, was on his way to superintend the summer work. He was tall, blonde, and quite handsome in his reserved fashion. He avoided company as much as possible, and when he was unavoidably drawn into conversation, he spoke with a quite derisive tone, so we left him alone as much as possible. Nonetheless, I couldn't help feeling that he was unhappy about something. One day he was standing by the rail, apparently lost in thought — not at all a pleasant thought, evidently. As I came along he gave me a slightly hostile stare. I glared right back at him and asked, "What makes you so disgusted with the world in general and me in particular? Do I remind you of someone you dislike?"

He was taken aback, and snapped, "Do you mean to say you are going to live up in this country?"

"Of course, for a few years at least," I replied.

"What! In this godforsaken place with no servants, or theatres, or shops or other conveniences!" He seemed to be quoting someone. "My dear young lady, are you in your right mind?"

His words were so filled with bitterness that I asked gently, "Is there anything strange in a girl wanting to live with her husband even up here?"

After a moment he answered mournfully, "The girls I know wouldn't do anything of the kind. They have to be cared for and pampered, dressed and manicured, and they would starve to death if they had to cook for themselves."

I was silent because I thought he must be thinking of some girl in particular, perhaps the one he wanted to marry. He continued abruptly, "Maybe I'm a little touchy on the subject, and maybe I'm just a little bit jealous of your husband. My girl just laughed when I asked her to marry me and come up here for the summer. She was going to the mountains back east, Adirondacks probably, where she will be going every summer while I come north to look after the mines."

"Dear me, how awful!" My voice was icy. "Am I supposed to be sorry for you? Why don't you come down off your pedestal sometime and meet some real girls. You don't *HAVE* to marry that kind, do you?"

He looked amazed for a moment, then shouted with laughter, the first time since he boarded the boat. Then he said, more soberly, "You know, maybe you're right! I don't really have to, do I? I'll remember this when I go back to San Francisco and do some looking around."

I was still feeling edgy and didn't smile. "There are many girls who have never known a sorority house, the Adirondacks or a house on Nob Hill; girls who have charm, beauty and loving hearts; girls who wouldn't know or care that your father has copper mines. Perhaps you could be loved for yourself alone?" I turned and left him, hoping that I had squared the account for some of my sister-hood and had given him something to think about. I must have been successful, because for the rest of the trip he was pleasant and cheerful.

The miners spoke so often about Manson Creek that I asked one of them to tell me about the place, how it was known by that name, and where it was. He seemed happy to tell the story. Gold had been found in the Babine country, but nothing very rich, he said. Then, in 1869, William Manson came from the Shetland Islands to Canada to make his fortune. For some reason, he chose to go to northern British Columbia and followed some prospectors up to the Babines where he started looking for gold. There are many little streams running into Babine Lake, and he selected one to stake his claim on, and there he was lucky. It was not long before he was finding gold, so he decided to stake another claim.

His claims turned out to be the richest found there; when word got out, the gold mining camp grew larger and larger until it was named Manson Creek.

"A lot of the men came from Barkerville, where there weren't many more claims left to stake," he continued, "and there were hundreds of men from all over the country looking for the lucky claim. Willie mined a lot of gold himself and then he sold out to a mining syndicate for more money than he ever dreamed of having. As soon as he was paid his money, he left the country and went back to the Shetland Islands, and we never saw him again." The sequel to this story was told me many years afterward by a man from the Shetlands, William Goodlet, and it deserves to be told in honour of that good man, Willie Manson.

When Manson returned to his home in Shetland, he saw the poverty and hard times among his people and decided to do something about it, according to Mr. Goodlet, who was born in the same village as William Manson, and was still living there when the transformation which followed Manson's return took place. Manson went to the highlands of Scotland's mainland and bought large flocks of sheep of the same breed as those in Shetland. He returned and sold them to the sheep farmers at cost and on long-term payments. Then he

The Skeena River, Hazelton, B.C.

built a woollen mill to process the wool, which was such a drudgery when it was done by hand. He employed some of the island's men and women to tend the sheep, while others worked in the mill, and some knitted garments from the mill's yarn. When he realized that there were too few skilled knitters to handle the output, he built a knitting mill, which gave employment to almost all the islanders, and the people prospered as they had never thought possible.

Mr. Goodlet, an old man by this time, had tears in his eyes as he finished his story and said, "To a Shetland Islander, his name is blessed. Wullie was the finest man in the land!"

Our week on the river was almost over and on Saturday evening we were in sight of our destination. As we docked, I could see Dan's head above the others waiting for us to disembark. I felt a moment of panic, knowing I was at last in the "Far Land," but I remembered that this was what I wanted, to see and learn about other places, and, having been born of a pioneering family, I drew a long breath and ran down the gangplank into Dan's arms.

CHAPTER THREE

Our
New Home

D AN, YOU DIDN'T EXPECT ME TODAY did you? You don't seem one bit surprised!"

"I'm not, Eve dear. I knew you wouldn't stay away from me any longer that you could help, so I was quite sure you would be on this boat!" He stopped his teasing tone, adding "if you hadn't been, I'd have gone to Rupert to get you."

It was wonderful to find the wharf solid and motionless under my feet. Columbus must have felt something of the same relief after his long voyage to discover America. Six days of climbing watery hills on a riverboat!

Dan had found a room, or rather a cubicle, in a rooming house, and after having coffee and doughnuts in a tiny café, he led me there.

The rooming house had originally been a five-room structure, but the housing shortage had prompted the owner to make it over into ten. Our room was so small I bumped my head on the ceiling getting into bed, and banged my knee on the knob of the dresser drawer getting out of it. The walls were building paper nailed on two-by-fours, so one could hear every whisper in the adjoining room. Believe me, I was shocked to the depths of my soul at what I heard. Dan smothered his chuckles, but my voice must have been heard because after a sudden silence a man's voice said "Hell, I forgot there was a woman in the house!"

Old Hazelton, May 1911. Ingenika Hotel in foreground.

I wondered what kind of place I had come to. I was aware that much the same kind of talk went on in my home town, but there it was in the privacy of a men's club or Masonic lodge, where the minister wouldn't hear. These men spoke of the natural functions of the body quite candidly and loudly, without any sign of furtiveness. Dan, whose life had been spent among such men, comforted me even while urging me to have a sense of humour.

Hazelton was a beautiful little town, thirteen acres in all, situated on a triangular strip of land between the junction of the Bulkley and Skeena Rivers, and the Gitanmaax Reservation. It was founded in the 1860s by an Englishman named Thomas Hankin, who saw the site's possibilities and left the employ of the Hudson's Bay Company to build his own trading post there. He received a land grant from the government and named the place Hazelton because of the profusion of hazel bushes everywhere around. The town was surrounded by mountains with snow on every peak and the hills across the river were dotted with jackpines. The sun was shining and everything looked bright to me the next morning as we went to the hotel for breakfast.

The Ingenika Hotel was owned by a man known from San Francisco to Dawson City as Black Jack, king of saloon keepers. The hotel was a two-storey frame building, unpainted and weather-beaten. The ground floor contained a seething mass of humanity walking in a thick fog of odours. From the bar, which ran the full length of the room, came the aroma of whiskey and beer, rum, and steam from the rinsing of glasses, while through the swinging doors at the rear came whiffs of food cooking. These, combined with the scent of tobacco smoke, made breathing an adventure. It was all so new and exciting to me that I was scarcely conscious of the strange smells, sights, and sounds.

We seated ourselves in a booth on the dining room side of the room and ordered ham, eggs, and coffee with toast. When they arrived, we found the ham and coffee excellent and the toast adequate, but my first bite of egg landed back on my plate. They were pale green in colour and so was I after that first bite. I am convinced they had been left over from the Yukon gold rush of 1898. Apart from the eggs, we enjoyed our breakfast, our first meal in the new land which was to be our home for several years.

The men who filled the place were mostly trappers just returned from their winter work in the mountains and valleys, and there were a few miners and prospectors who had not yet left for the hills and their claims for the summer season. Some were men from the construction gangs building the railroad grade, who were camped not far from town.

As soon as we finished breakfast, Dan took me up the low hill at the back of the town to the enclosure in which he had erected the tent. It was on the Kitimax Reserve, the home of the Hazelton tribe of the Gitanmaax. We had several white neighbours, because the town was so overcrowded that all newcomers had to rent space from the Natives. They were glad to let the white people use their buildings, as it brought them a few dollars to alleviate their desperate poverty.

Hazelton was a typical northern village, with log cabins of all sizes, tents and a few larger houses belonging to the merchants and government employees. Along the short main street were high-fronted log buildings in which the town's business was conducted. There were three hotels, a couple of cafés, a real estate office, a printing office, a drug store, and three large trading posts. There was a primitive air about the place, although it had been in existence for at least fifty years. I told myself, "Well, Eva, this is what you wanted, isn't it? To find out how other people live in other places? Here it is, so make the best of it."

As we walked toward the tent Dan said, "See that big white house, there's a very nice woman living there, and she has been most helpful. She lends me tools and one day she brought me some coffee, and sat down and we talked for a while. I think you'll like her."

"What does she look like?"

"Oh, she isn't very pretty and not exactly young, but she has lovely blonde hair, and she's as friendly as can be."

As we passed through our neighbour's yard, I looked at Dan with a derisive smile. On the clothesline fluttered two blonde wigs, freshly shampooed.

Dan's face was a mixture of amazement and disillusionment. "Well, she was friendly anyway, and you can't judge a woman by her hair!"

Our tent had a board floor and three-foot walls of green lumber, which later dried, leaving wide spaces between the boards. Our fourteen-by-twenty-four tent was laced down over the framework and a tent fly fastened a few inches above the canvas formed a roof. It was all new and bright, it was our first home, and we loved it. We went to work immediately to unpack the boxes and trunks which arrived with me.

That afternoon we had our first visitors, the Reverend John Field and Mrs. Field, and their house guest, Archbishop Du Vernet, who was touring his diocese which included Hazelton. The archbishop was a charming guest and told us many stories of the country around us. The Fields were celebrating their twenty-fifth year in Hazelton as missionaries, and I couldn't help wondering what the reaction would be in my parental home when my letter with this news arrived, together with my request that they tell our worried minister that there were more churches and missions per capita in Hazelton than in his own town.

I decided to try to make tea for them, as I had a teacaddy filled with tea in my crate of wedding presents, and there were plenty of cups and saucers. The only thing lacking was hot water, and I decided to go to my neighbour and ask for some, which of course, would give me a chance to see her. She opened the door as soon as I knocked and said, "Oh, you must be Mrs. MacLean! Come right in, I'm so glad to see you!"

Her handshake was firm and warm and her face was beaming with friendliness. Ashamed of my earlier doubts, I asked her if she could let me have some hot water to make tea for my guests.

"I surely will, my dear, all you want." She filled my teapot and opened her cupboard door. "Here, take this plate of cookies, I just took them out of the oven and they are still warm. I'm so glad you came over because I was wondering if there was anything I could do to make you feel welcome."

My face was burning and there was almost a lump in my throat as I thanked her and invited her to come and see us as soon as we were settled. Dan was right: you couldn't judge a woman by her hair, even it if was a wig.

My new friend's name was Marie Williams, and her husband Hank was out in the hills prospecting for the summer. They had been in the Yukon in 1898, where Hank had been a gambling miner and she had been a dance hall girl. When the gold rush had faded, they were married and had come to live in Hazelton.

I was bewildered. There was I, living next door to one of those women folks back home had been wont to mention in whispers. She hadn't any horns, and after that first meeting, for me she wore a halo. I was thankful to be living next door to her, rather than a Mrs. Elmer Baxter.

For the first week, we stayed in our tiny room at night, ate our meals at the hotel, and spent the rest of the time getting acquainted with the townspeople and surrounding country. On Thursday, the day before the archbishop was to leave for the coast, he invited us to be his dinner guests at the hotel, and we accepted gladly. He was congenial company and had taught us much about the customs and history of our new home.

As we approached the hotel that day at noon, the iron triangle dinner gong rang out its invitation. Dogs of all kinds swarmed all over the place; thin, mangy looking malamutes and huskies, most of them with several other breeds somewhere in their blood. The archbishop said, with a smile, "Don't mind the dogs, they always howl like that when they hear the dinner gong. One day an old prospector yelled at them, 'Shut up! You don't have to eat here, what are you howling for!'"

After several days of eating in that hotel, we sympathized heartily with both men and dogs. Everything on the table tasted much the same — meat, vegetables, and pie — as though everything had been cooked in the same pan. It wasn't exactly appetizing.

Shortly after being seated at our table and giving our order, we became vaguely conscious of voices in the adjoining booth. There was only a low partition dividing us from its occupants, and we could easily hear their conversation.

Two miles from town was a small cluster of cabins where several prostitutes lived. These women were in and out of town almost every day, and on this occasion two of them were being entertained at dinner by a couple of railway workers. In a lull in our own conversation their voices floated out clearly. We gathered that another of their sorority had wanted to come with them but was not permitted to do so. A man's voice said, "Aw, why didn't you bring her along? She's not half bad!"

A shrill soprano answered, "Say, if that cheap five-dollar bitch thinks she can travel with us she's crazy!"

Dan and I stared at each other with open-mouthed wonder. The archbishop's eyes were twinkling as he said, softly, "Strange isn't it, how the problem of class distinction seems to enter all walks of life!"

We smothered our laughter as well as we could and continued our meal, trying not to hear any more of the conversation next door.

Two days later, another boat arrived from the coast and with it came our furniture, at least what was left of it. My kitchen cabinet had lost a leg, and the glass in the doors was broken. I almost wept when I found the little wicker rocking chair we bought with such care no longer had any rockers. But we lost no time in having the furniture delivered to the tent, and then we went to work getting the essentials in place as we thought we had spent enough time in the tiny bedroom, and eating at the hotel.

It was thrilling to get our little sheet iron stove set up and our own bed to sleep in. In the limited space at our disposal, we were forced to place the bedspring on top of a couple of rows of boxes on the floor. Dan unpacked his books, putting them in the bookcase which had to perch on top of the desk. He hung his riding paraphernalia, including his saddle, on the wall in the tent's bedroom area and we used the dresser as a screen to hide the bed. Our table, chairs, and a comfortable couch were placed in the centre section. We partitioned off the six feet left at the front of the tent with building paper on upright posts for our kitchen, and there we placed the remains of the cabinet, a few shelves for our groceries, and the stove, one of the smallest I had ever seen. These were snug living quarters, but warm and very comfortable.

Now came the battle of food. Coming from the Ontario farm, I didn't know anything about canned, dehydrated or smoke-cured food, but I certainly learned about it that first year. We ate canned vegetables, tomatoes and corn being about all we could get in those days; canned bluenose butter from Nova Scotia, canned fruit, dried fruit, and dehydrated potatoes. I baked with egg powder rather than risk the waterglassed eggs, which had been stored for many a day. Fanny and Mother were always sending me recipes from home, but since most of them began, "take three or four eggs," I asked them to stop as it was impossible to obtain even one fresh egg.

I baked beans and we ate them with ham on Monday, bacon on Tuesday, canned salmon or bully beef on Wednesday, and we repeated the process week after week, until we had forgotten there was such a thing as fresh food in the world. My neighbour, Marie, taught me a good deal about making appetizing dishes from leftovers mixed with some of the canned delicacies. These special foods cost a fortune at the trading post, but they did make life more pleasant.

I learned many things from Marie. She was lonely with Hank away most of the time, and she lived very quietly and carefully, as there were a few women among the newcomers who watched her every move in the hope that she would break loose and resume her former occupation at any moment. She was determined to prove that she was as respectable as they. My early training had given me the idea that things were either black or white, but this rigidity of outlook was softening, and shades of colour were beginning to appear in my mental picture. Almost at the same time, these women criticized me for associating with Marie, my Irish temper rose, and in my resentment I said many things an older and wiser person would have avoided. This proved to me what I had long known: that I would never be a "proper" minister's wife because I was too rebellious, a characteristic frowned upon by religionists.

Dan, too, was finding out that all was not always smooth sailing for men of the church. Missionaries were not popular with northern men, and for this there was some excuse, although he didn't have to worry very long. Dan's early success had been because he did not look like a parson, dress like a parson, or talk like one, but that success became permanent when the local male residents discovered he was able to do something which they admired as being useful work.

The boat which brought Dan to Hazelton from the coast also gave passage to a fine team of horses which were to be used on the railway supply line. One of the horses developed enteritis and was desperately ill. Dan, of course, offered his services as a veterinarian, worked night and day over the animal, and had the satisfaction of seeing it recover completely. The men on the boat were amazed to see a minister who was also a veterinarian, and promptly named him "Doc." It was disconcerting for me to see how much more respect they offered him after this event. To those rugged frontiersmen, a man who could save a good horse's life was more worthy of respect than one who spent his time trying to save souls. Few of them felt any worry whatever on that

Dan on "Teddy", a company horse (Foley, Welsh & Stewart).

Dan and Eva in their new home in Old Hazelton.

latter score, but a man who could put that horse back on its feet again was worthwhile, because, as they said, "that horse was sure sick."

Soon after we were settled in our tent, the construction company offered Dan the job of taking care of the horses and mules used in the building of the railroad. He accepted willingly because he knew he would have a great deal more influence over the men as a veterinarian and doctor than as a minister. His creed was principle rather than dogma, cleanliness above holiness, and he gained their liking and respect more quickly in the barns watching over their sick horses than he could ever do from a pulpit. (Not that any of them ever went to church!)

Then came the long summer evenings when the sun was high in the sky until after ten o'clock. We used to go for long walks northward on a trail which led us along the brow of the river's high banks. Wild roses bloomed in such profusion that the hillside was a pink haze as far as the eye could distinguish colour. We wandered through the old Native cemetery, with its tiny houses built over the graves, and down to the Bulkley River at the junction with the Skeena.

Five minutes from town, and we were as much alone as though there was nobody else in the world, with a silence was so great that it almost made one's ears ache. To stand on the top of a hill with that beautiful country at one's feet, and with magnificent mountains reaching far up into the blue sky, was to feel as though one were floating through space and there was no such thing as time.

Dan said, one evening when we were looking out across the river to the hills beyond, "I'm glad we came, aren't you? I feel so alive!"

"And I'm very glad you're still alive," I said. "I thought for a minute this morning I was going to be a widow."

"This morning? Was I in danger? What are you talking about?"

I asked if he remembered when we were down at the trading post getting our groceries. "There were two women standing next to you at the counter, and one of them dropped her parasol. Know who they were?"

"Sure! Girls from Two-mile. What of it?"

"You picked up the parasol and bowed and smiled so politely when you gave it to her. I thought the Lord would strike you dead. He did Ananias in for telling a little fib, and there you were, speaking to and smiling at a pair of prostitutes."

Dan was laughing, "You idiot!" But I was thoughtful.

"You know the old Presbyterians would have had you up before the Session if they saw you doing anything except praying for them, and you were treating them as politely as if they were members of the Ladies Aid. Some parson you are!"

"You're as bad as I am," he countered, "I saw you talking to two of them this morning when you were hanging out your clothes. What were you talking about?"

"At first I was just listening to them because I was interested in what they were saying. They were waiting for the stage just outside the fence, and I heard one of them say, 'Migod! These are hard times, not like they used to be. Too many married women in this town.'"

"Sure are. We can't compete with a free lunch counter."

43

"While I was wondering what on earth she meant, the tall one said, 'They say there's a veterinarian in town. Wonder if he could do anything for Fifi, she's the sickest little dog I ever saw.'"

"But he's a parson! You can't take her to him can you?"

Then I walked over to them and said, "My husband, Dr. MacLean, is the veterinarian and I'm sure he would be glad to do anything he can for your little dog. Do bring her in."

They looked surprised and embarrassed, but one of them said, "Thank you, Mrs. MacLean, we'll bring her in in the morning."

"So you see, Mr. Doc, you'll have visitors in the morning. I almost forgot to tell you. I just hope none of our good church ladies see them coming in." Dan just chuckled and led the way back down the hill.

Next morning, the stage stopped outside our tent and the two women alighted, one of them carrying the little dog in her arms as they walked to the door.

Little Fifi was in the final stage of pneumonia and died before Dan could do anything for her. Lily sobbed bitterly as she told us, "She was the only thing I had that really loved me or that I loved." We felt sorry for her. I insisted on making them a cup of tea, and while they were drinking it, Blanche, the taller woman, probably in her early thirties, told us she had a little daughter in Seattle, who thought her mother was a dressmaker. "Another couple of hundred in the bank and that's what I'll be and I hope she never knows different," she said.

Strangely enough, we wished her luck.

CHAPTER FOUR

Getting
Acquainted

Hazelton was a busy little town in the summertime, but the old-timers told us we hadn't seen anything yet. They said, "Wait till the miners and prospectors come in for the winter and then the place will really hum." We began to wonder when we would sleep if the winter was busier than the summer.

There were only some twenty white families in town, and many single men and others, like ourselves, recently arrived. The Native population was about five hundred. The three hotels, the Ingenika, Omineca, and the Hazelton, all did a roaring business, and the three trading posts owned by the Hudson's Bay Company and sourdoughs Cunningham and Sargent were equally prosperous.

It didn't take long to become acquainted with everyone and suddenly the little town was home. Our church service was held at first in the dance hall, and when we were singing the hymns on Sundays, I sometimes fancied I could hear the ghostly sound of the pioneers' feet rapping to keep time with the handorgan or violin music.

Beside our tent in the enclosure there was a small log cabin which was occupied by miners in the winter and trappers in the summer. It was never vacant for a day throughout the year, and there were always so many men coming and going that I was unable to see how they could all crowd into such a small space.

Harry Davies, one of the prospectors living there, was soon to retire, and he was hoping to sell his claim. Welsh by birth, Davies was a short stout man with a white beard and hair, and a sunny smile which made him appear younger than his hair and beard suggested. He often visited me while I worked, telling me stories about the country when he dug for gold in the Omineca Hills. One evening I invited him and his two partners, Hugh and Tom McKay, for supper. They accepted gladly as this was the first time they had been invited to supper at a home since they had been in the country. Harry Davies approached me and asked shyly if he could bring someone with him. I told him he was quite welcome to do so.

"I've an old friend I used to know in Wales, and he's passing through on his way to have a look at what's left of the Manson Creek gold mining camp, and I think you would enjoy meeting him," explained Davies. "He's from Barkerville in the Cariboo and his name is Harry Jones. A fine man he is."

"Of course, bring him along," I said. "We'll be glad to have him."

The four of them arrived and we met the stranger, a man of medium height, and slight of build, but we soon discovered that he possessed a strong and virile personality. During dinner, we all enjoyed listening to the two Welsh friends indulging in memories of their early lives in Wales. When Davies teased Jones about rumours of some girl, Harry Jones just shook his head and smiled gently.

After supper, we gathered around the little heater in the tent's living room, and Harry Davies took his pipe from his pocket, then looked expectantly at me. I responded, "Go ahead, light up and smoke if you wish; we like to see men comfortable."

Harry Jones hastily produced his pipe and said, "You're very kind, lass, and thank you." He lit his pipe, then looked thoughtfully at me and said, "You know, you look much like the girl Harry was talking about. She was a fine plump lassie. None of your skinny ones for me!" I didn't know whether I liked that or not, but at least she was "fine."

"You know, if I hadn't been such a shy, speechless lump when I was young," he continued, "I might have had a daughter about your age, maybe even a grandchild, instead of being a lonely man without anybody close to me."

"Weren't you ever married, Mr. Jones? Surely you must have loved some one when you were young?" I asked.

"No, I'm just an old bachelor," he replied, then added quietly, "Would you like to hear about my only romance? It was pretty hard then, but it's a long time ago. I've never told anyone about it before, but you've set me thinking about her."

Dan spoke up quickly, "We'll enjoy hearing your story, Mr. Jones, you may be sure." The others echoed him while Harry Davies said not a word. He seemed to be saddened somehow, as though he knew the story.

The pipe had gone out and Jones reached for another match, lit it, and held it motionless in his fingers while he sat lost in his memories.

"It was many years ago, when I was just a lad, that I first saw the lass. Her family moved to our part of the country and settled on a small farm about a mile from the village. There was a low hill between, and when I walked to the top of it I could look down on her house. I used to watch her light go out many times." He smoked silently for a few minutes.

"Every Sunday she came to the chapel in the village and I'd walk along not far away and watch her chattering to her friends as they passed by. Her hair was pure gold, and her face, well, to me it was the prettiest face in the whole world. Some of the other lads used to tease me about her, but if I met her face to face, I couldn't even lift my head for my shyness, and I was so dumbstruck I could not even say 'good-day.' So nearly every night I would go to the top of the hill, and make up my mind to go right down to the house and knock on the door and ask to see her. But I never did!"

Another lighting of the pipe, and he continued, "This went on for nearly three years. You were on your way to the Omineca, Davies, and didn't know her, but still I hadn't spoken to her. I watched her face and listened to her merry laugh. More than once she had glanced at me — kindly, I thought — but I still got red in the face and overcome with my shyness every time she was near."

His eyes were looking far back into the past and when he spoke his voice, was soft, "One day I heard that she was to marry another lad, and that night when I went to the hilltop I saw them come out, hand-in-hand, and stroll across the field toward the village. I cried that night for the first time since I was a wee lad and my mother had punished me. Two months after the wedding, I was on my way to Canada and the Barkerville gold fields. I never married, though, because even after I lost my dumb shyness, it was her face I could see every time I looked at a woman." After a moment, he added softly, "And I had never even spoken to my love."

We all sat silent, in the spell of the saddest love story I had ever heard. My eyes were full of tears as I went to make coffee. I thought we needed it. Over the steaming cups we recovered our spirits and the evening ended in happier conversation. I asked Harry Jones if he couldn't tell us another story, something a little less sad, and he said, smiling, "I could tell you a story about my ambitious aunt and her daughter, my cousin."

Harry Davies laughed. "I remember your aunt and her pretty daughter, and often wondered if she ever found a man good enough to be her son-in-law."

"She did indeed. She wouldn't let her daughter have anything to do with the village lads, said they weren't what she planned for the girl. When she couldn't find anyone good enough there, she was going to move to the city where there would be men who would be worthy of the girl. Then before she left, something happened. A young fellow came to town and opened a law office and began his practice. My aunt got excited right away, and the first Sunday, after chapel, she invited him home to have supper with them. The young lawyer, who was just as ambitious as my aunt, accepted eagerly. That was the start, and soon the two young people were seen together everywhere. Next thing we knew they were getting married. Before long they moved to the city and the last I heard before I left, they were getting along and up in the world, and he was going to go into politics."

Our friends left then, Harry Jones to the hotel, and the others to their cabin next door.

Twenty-two years late, I met Harry Jones again. This time he was a mere shadow of his former self. He had been seriously ill in the Quesnel hospital for several weeks, and he was now recuperating at the Australian Ranch, home of his friend of many years, Jack Yorston. I happened to be visiting the ranch at the same time, and was delighted to renew my acquaintance with him. To my surprise, he remembered me and told the others about having supper with Dan and me in the tent in Hazelton. He looked steadily at me for a moment and asked, "Didn't I tell you about the girl I loved when I was young? I remember the tears in your eyes when you saw my memories were unhappy. I didn't forget that either, and you're still a bonny lass."

His words almost brought the tears again, this time because he looked so frail and tired. Harry Jones was a well-known and highly respected man throughout the Cariboo country, and he had once served as the area's Conservative member in the British Columbia Legislature in Victoria.

As we sat comfortably resting after supper in the big livingroom, I asked him if he remembered telling us about his ambitious aunt and her pretty daughter. "Tell me, did she and her son-in-law ever achieve their ambition to be successful? Who was he?"

Harry's eyes were twinkling with mischief as he answered, "Well, you might say he climbed a bit. You see, the young lawyer's name was David Lloyd George!"

We were all completely astonished. Even his old friend Jack had not known that.

Some months after this meeting, we received a telephone message from Harry Jones' nephew, who lived in Vancouver, that his uncle had come to make his home with him and his family, and that he wanted to see us. He and Dan had become good friends while we were living in Quesnel 1915 to 1920, although I did not see him during those years because he had been living in his cabin not far from Barkerville, and rarely came to Quesnel.

We were so glad to hear he was living in Vancouver that we went to visit him that same afternoon. Although he was still frail physically, in spirit he was as sprightly as ever, and he greeted us warmly. As he shook hands with me he said, "Ah, the bonny lass from Hazelton."

He died soon after we saw him, much mourned by his former constituents in the northern Cariboo.

CHAPTER FIVE

Baseball
and
Beef

ALL THROUGH THAT SUMMER, Dan brought miners, trappers, or drifters home with him for supper. It was flattering to me, of course, to hear so many praises of my cooking, but the time came when I hated the sight of a biscuit or a pie. My sheet iron stove never had a chance to cool off. When the Labour Day holiday came around, I warned Dan that I would not cook for anyone other than ourselves for once. I was going to enjoy the sports programme, I told him, and he could eat anything he could find when supper time came. I didn't know we were going to have an unexpected feast.

The next morning we were up early and off to the main street where the morning sports were to be held. There were foot races for men, women and children, in which both Natives and whites participated, a tug-of-war and, afterwards, some horse racing. This was exciting as the entries included some former racehorses from the south, as well as fast Native ponies.

One Native, known as "The Salmon," from a neighbouring reserve rode a big, bony sorrel which was more or less unmanageable. Whether the man had earned this soubriquet from his reddish complexion and receding chin, or whether it was a free translation of his name, I have no idea. But he certainly was unable to keep the unruly animal under control. I remember that he kept us all in a high state of nervousness, as the sorrel dashed around along the track

Baseball field in Old Hazelton, where K'San Village and Campsite is today.

or into the crowd that lined the street, just as the animal fancied. Some of his sudden plunges caused the spectators to scatter in every direction until the rider was able to get his mount under control.

But these events were merely preliminary to the main sport of the day, the afternoon baseball game. The ball field was on a level stretch of meadow below the Second Bench, which was on the reserve, and this was the prettiest setting for a ball game one could find anywhere. The teams competing were players from the construction camps against players from the valley and the village. Everyone living within a distance of fifty miles attended the game which started at 1:30. The money wagered on the teams that day would have built a couple of miles of railroad. The air was black with hats thrown skyward at every good play, regardless of which side made it, and the shouts of the fans were deafening as the game went on. In the eighth inning the score was even, three men on bases, and Jim Riley, the Babe Ruth of the home team, was just picking up his bat on his way to the mound. He waved it around to acknowledge the cheers from the bleachers, and stepped up to the plate. The pitcher was warming up for the crucial throw; the crowd fell silent. Jim struck a home run and the score went soaring. But no one saw the miracle.

In the silence before the ball left the pitcher's hand, a man came running past the crowd in the bleachers, shouting, "Beef! Pat Burns's drive is in and there's beef at the butcher shop!"

The crowd rose to its feet as one man and surged towards the village. They ran, puffing, feeling in their pockets to make sure they had some money left after all the betting, all thought of the ball game washed from their minds. Fans of today can thank their stars they were never as hungry for fresh meat as we were then. When the crowd reached the shop, the line formed to the right, and each waited his turn. Only one old cow had been butchered, but Dan's long legs had given him a head start on others in the crowd, so we were fortunate enough to receive two pounds of round steak. When the last ounce of the cow was sold there was still a long line waiting. What pleading looks they turned on their more fortunate friends! But as two pounds was the limit to any one customer, the friends clutched their treasure to their bosoms and fled with averted eyes. As the last customer left the shop, the butcher sank, exhausted, on the bench.

The unsuccessful would-be purchasers returned to the ball field to find the game over and the players all gone. There were bets to be collected on the winning home team, but nobody seemed to care! Those with meat hurried home to cook it, while the others were so disappointed they seemed to forget all about the game. The players had, with one accord, assembled at the bar of the nearest hotel to celebrate their victory, soften their defeat, or drown their chagrin at being deserted at the mere mention of beef.

And such beef! The drive had travelled overland from the Chilcotin in the Cariboo district, hundreds of miles away; it had been weeks on the trail, and all the better carcasses had been purchased by the construction camps before reaching Hazelton. There had been nothing left but one old, tired cow, and its meat could be better imagined than described. But it was fresh meat, and the gravy, at least, was good.

Another wave of excitement had swept the town just before the Labour Day

A banquet held to honour P.E. Sands, and the first automobile to enter Hazelton by the overland route.

holiday. It had been rumoured that an automobile was to come to Hazelton by the overland trail from the south coast. To some of the older men who had followed that trail to the Manson Creek gold fields, and found it almost impassable for pack mules or even for men on foot, this was nonsense. They said it couldn't be done. But it was done, and one day late in August a Flanders 20 drove into town and came to a halt in front of the Hazelton Hotel. The town's entire population rushed to see this wonder. The car owner, P. E. Sands, and his two mechanics were greeted with loud cheers, and that night a great celebration was held in the hotel dining room to which all the town's white men were invited. The so-called "second class citizens" (the white women and the Natives) were excluded, although the Natives, unrestrained by cultural barriers, were particularly excited to see a "wagon which went without horses," and gathered in crowds to examine it while the banquet was in progress inside.

The car's journey had taken several weeks and its drivers had been faced with almost insurmountable difficulty, Mr. Sands told men attending the celebratory dinner. In places, they had to take the car apart and load it on the backs of mules borrowed from a packtrain, to be carried over rushing streams. But they had completed their journey, and proudly they had driven in triumph down the street of Hazelton. They returned to Prince Rupert by riverboat, and from there to Vancouver by steamer. But the excitement of baseball, fresh meat, and the arrival of an automobile overland was only a prelude to the biggest event of all before this year was out.

In November a federal election was to be held, when the main issue was reciprocity between Canada and the United States. Politically, the town was almost equally divided, with one party in favour of free trade, while the other wanted none of it. Something had to be done, and since Black Jack belonged to the party which abhorred the thought of free trade, he decided to do what was required to stop it.

He was a friend of the provincial attorney-general, and he frequently boasted that he could get any permit he wanted, so he had no hesitation about bending a few laws such as the one about closing the bars the night before the election. He then announced that on the evening before the big day, drinks would be on the house, from nine o'clock to midnight. Few of the men were at all displeased about this, and proceeded to take advantage of his generous offer, while the women stayed indoors; they weren't able to vote anyway, so they ignored the whole matter.

When the bar closed at midnight, the police took over, and with a couple of deputies they began to clear the streets. Soon the jail was filled to capacity, although not more than half the men from the bar were picked up. The others were taken home and carefully put to bed, so they would be in good condition to vote the next morning.

The polls opened and closed, and the votes were counted. The result was amazing! Only a handful of votes were cast for reciprocity, all the rest were against it, and Hazelton had done its best to save the country from disaster. The men in the jail had been sentenced to three days for being drunk and disorderly in a public place. They were released the morning of the third day. They were the angriest men in all the North, and there was nothing they could do about it.

CHAPTER SIX

Of
Native Culture
and
Ceremonials

Since our tent was pitched on the reserve, we were in close contact with the Native people. At home in Ontario I had known the Ojibwas and the Chippewas, while Dan was more familiar with the Cree and Blackfoot of the plains. I learned that the upper Skeena Natives were Gitanmaax, Carriers, Babines, and other tribes to the north. As I came to know them better, I discovered they had one thing in common with Natives of eastern Canada, the women did most of the work. Of course, this is not an exclusively Native characteristic, it has been noticed elsewhere in the world!

The Native women made baskets, blankets, moccasins, jackets, and rugs, trading them to white people for cast-off clothing and food from the stores. They came to our door regularly, making a great clatter outside to bring me out to see them and their wares. One old woman used to sit down on the doorstep and, drawing her shawl over head, would moan lustily, "Memaloose all papoose (all my children are dead), want cup-a-tea." This she would repeat over and over until I gave her a cup of tea to quiet her weeping. I felt sorry for her at first, believing that her children had actually left her to starve. She said her coffin was all ready for her, but someone must feed her until she died. Then I learned that the old women are actually very important members of the tribe, and wield much power. She looked exceedingly well-fed and had plenty of

Hazelton Natives pose for the camera.

clothing wrapped around her, so I thought she was attempting to fool me. However, she wasn't any worse than the multitude of agents, salesmen and other annoying callers one has anywhere, and she may have learned her methods by studying these white men.

The Native women were excellent basketmakers, and they dyed their wares most artistically. We had baskets of all sizes for everything that needed a receptacle, some acquired in exchange for some item we no longer needed. For example, I was able to trade one of my older dresses for a rabbit skin blanket.

One morning, as I was washing my breakfast dishes, I thought I could hear the sound of a brass band, which grew louder as I listened. I ran outside to see if any of my neighbours could hear it too; as I had seen so many strange things, I was prepared for a musical mirage. And then I saw it! The band was following a funeral procession up the long trail to the top of the hill known as the Second Bench. It rose high above the plateau called the First Bench, where we lived. On top of this Second Bench was the Native cemetery. The rhythm and harmonies of the music were quite new to me, and so strange were the sounds

Native cemetery.

that the effect was at once chilling and charming. Then the procession disappeared over the brow of the hill and the music died away. About an hour later I heard the band again, this time playing lively martial music loudly and vigorously. The procession was winding back down the hill along the road to the village from which it came.

Later it was explained to me that the slow, mournful music of the ascent was intended to express the Natives' grief at the loss of a member of the tribe. I remember thinking they must have loved him very much to inspire such doleful sounds. The lively music played on the descent was to frighten away any evil spirits which might be hovering around, and make them think that nobody was buried in the newly covered grave.

After supper that night Dan and I went up the hill to see this cemetery of which we had heard many times. We found it to be a real "village of the dead," as the Natives called it. It was nicely laid out in streets and lanes that were lined with grave houses of fantastic shapes and decorations. There were trees, flowers, and green grass forming a restful background for the vivid colouring of the houses. Some had roofs, others had only four walls with barbaric spikes and clusters of carved wood at the corners. They all had windows and some of them had mirrors in the doors as well. Inside were the belongings of the deceased, their tools, dishes, clothing, and here and there were photographs. One house had a long hank of hair hanging from the roof, honouring the woman from whose head it had been cut, for long hair was a mark of distinction.

Some Natives having a slight acquaintanceship with Christianity, had also placed tombstones by the graves, reasoning that it would be well to be on the safe side in case their souls fell into the hands of an unfamiliar god. To them, our God was a very strange character. There was something gloriously peaceful about this village of the dead, this cemetery so well-kept and beautiful. The homes of the living Natives, by contrast, were often untidy, dusty, and bare because their inhabitants lived in abject poverty. The comparison reminded us of the way white men build monuments, cairns, peace arches, and cenotaphs in honour of dead heroes, while often the living are condemned to slums, jungles, and tenements.

One morning in November we were awakened by the sound of tom-toms and singing which heralded a festival, potlatch, or celebration, at which local Natives were entertaining neighbouring tribes. This was an event which took place only seldom, because it depended largely on the prosperity of the tribe whose turn it was to entertain. The year past had been fairly prosperous as the fish and game had been plentiful. This festival was being held in a field right across from our tent, so we had a ringside seat.

A large bonfire had been lighted, and the crowd gathered, clan after clan, greeted fraternally by the chief and other head men of the tribe. For three days the Natives danced, sang and visited each other, taking time out only for feasting and sleep. Men, women and children were dressed in strange and varied costumes, representing all the birds and animals of their totems, the more extravagant and unique the better. Some of the costumes were fantastic both in design and material. For example, one man's garb was fashioned to resemble a tree, his arms at right angles, like branches. His costume of brown and green was dotted from top to toe with one dollar bills, probably the savings of many years. While they lasted, these bills were given out as gifts to the visitors as this man's contribution to the general celebration. As I passed by on my tour of the grounds, I was rather embarrassed that he insisted on giving one bill to me. I thanked him, shook his extended hand, and he was assured that I was his friend.

Most of the headdresses and masks were symbols of their respective clans, painted and carved into mythical figures used on their totems. Some costumes were of brightly dyed feathers, while one was made entirely of rabbit paws. Others were made of bright calico with bits of tin, coloured glass, and beads sewn all over them.

Around the fire the tribes gathered, some seated, others walking up and down, or standing motionless. From ten to twenty dancers took turns in the centre of the ring, moving in monotonous rhythm, while the others sang, or beat their drums.

The music's slow wail, the drumbeat, and the steady movement of the dancing feet had a hypnotic effect, and for a moment we white spectators were swayed by the primitive spirit which is dormant in all people.

Now and then a dancer would approach the small group of white spectators, but as we were unacquainted with the proper procedure on such occasions, we smiled, shook hands frequently, asked questions, and laughed with them. They seemed satisfied that we were friendly.

The evening feasts were held in the "big house" which was used as a community centre and council chamber. I was so deeply interested in the whole affair that I asked two of my neighbours to go with me to get a glimpse of the festivities. We asked a couple of the Natives who were standing outside for permission to enter, and they gave most cordial consent. We went just inside but no further. The feast was nearly over and the heat was unbearable. Smoke from the oil lamps combined almost overpoweringly with the odour of smoked salmon, oolichan oil, and other delicacies. The noise was terrific, but we stayed for a while to see as much as possible of their rites and ceremonies.

In the centre of the room a sick man was marched up and down, supported on either side by his brothers, while in front of him a medicine man danced and writhed, moaning and shaking his hand rattle. One Native woman told us he was trying to keep evil spirits away from the sick man, and I was inclined to believe his activities might be highly effective. No spirit, good or bad, could be hero enough to brave the sight and sound of the medicine man. Whether the sick man recovered or not, I do not know, because our visit came to an abrupt end when the shaman looked straight at me and loosed a horrible yell as he passed by. He may have thought I was an evil spirit; we didn't stay to argue the matter, but fled into the night.

A few days later the storm broke over my head. The daughter of the missionary from "Heaven" visited us. I knew her quite well as she had visited me several times, but I was not prepared for the shower of criticism which fell from her lips when she heard we had attended the potlatch. My husband was out at the time, so I was sole recipient of the lecture.

"The very idea of you, the wife of a Christian minister, attending and countenancing such rites! I am certainly surprised at you, you should know better! It is people like you who undo all the good work which we have done among the Native people. . . ." she ranted on. But when she said we were encouraging them in their heathenish practices, I exploded into speech.

"I suppose it is all right to encourage them in *OUR* heathenish practices! A good many white people do, it seems. We've taught them to lie, to steal, to drink whiskey; their women have been defiled and their homes broken up. If our particular brand of religion is so shaky it won't stand up against their picnic, then there's something awfully wrong with it."

I could not understand what harm the Natives were doing unless the shaman's performance could be called antisocial. But what of the antics of some of our own medicine men? They do not always heal, and many of their practices, even when well meant, puzzle the unenlightened laity very much.

The Native feast of smoked fish, dried berries, and oolichan oil might not have appealed to our jaded appetites, but they in turn might not have enjoyed a green salad, hot dogs, or ice cream. As for their dancing, has anyone watched a conga line, a jitterbug performance, or perhaps a rock and roll session?

Native gift exchanges have their counterpart in our Christmas orgy today, which is just a commercialized potlatch, an excessive spending of hard-earned money with little spirit of love about it. And when it comes to romance, they are similar to many we all know — guided as much by hardheaded reason as by their hearts. I discovered this fact a few days after the celebration.

My missionary friend had departed in a state of extreme agitation and I expected to find myself explaining my sins to the Presbytery. But I heard no more about the matter, so perhaps our earlier friendship cooled her anger somewhat. Or it may have been that the Natives, many of whom belonged to her father's village, would not have approved of any trouble caused by their Hazelton friends. It was a case of discretion being better than valour.

The enclosure in which we lived belonged to the head of the Hazelton tribe, Chief John. His family, and the four white families living there, were the only people allowed to take water from the well, which was beside our tent. I had become fairly well acquainted with the chief's wife, a young, pleasant and neatly dressed woman, the mother of a little boy about five years old. She was always friendly and liked to chat a little while when she came for water. She spoke good English, as she had been sent to a mission school at Port Essington when she was a child. The boy was shy, but he made friends with Dan after he had washed and bandaged a cut in the child's foot.

One morning after the potlatch, I went out to the well for water and found, to my infinite dismay, a fat, middle-aged Native woman and several small children who were paddling around the top of the well in their moccasined feet. Being quite sure they had no right to come there for water, I said, "You cannot get water from this well, only the white people and the chief's family can use this well. There are plenty of other wells on the reserve, so you must go away."

She glared at me and muttered, "I no go way. I get water!"

When I repeated my demand, she just grunted, "I go way now, but I come back soon."

In a few minutes she was back, accompanied by the chief, who smiled at me and explained, "This is my new wife! I get her from Chief Martin at

Native salmon trap at Hazelton, B.C.

potlatch. She got many sons to catch fish by and by. Pretty soon I have much salmon stored and I be rich man!"

I was so astounded I could scarcely find my voice to apologize to the new wife. Then I fled into the tent to ponder on this strange Native custom. This was one of the sins the missionary's daughter had so strongly condemned. I told her that trading wives was a white man's custom long before the Natives had heard of it. The difference was that since the white courts had been established, wife exchanges had been conducted with the aid of legal procedures, while large fees were collected by members of the legal profession. Indeed, some of our forebearers had not traded their wives away, but had them beheaded in order to make way for a new wife. Natives, on the other hand, had acted according to their own laws, which gave permission for such a trade if both parties agreed. The question was, which method was more civilized?

One could not live in the north country very long without seeing plainly what white civilization had done to the Natives. White men had brought such "refining" influences as whiskey, thievery, adultery, syphilis, and tuberculosis to the tribes, and they had systematically robbed the Natives at the same time.

The missionaries had tried to demolish the foundations of the Natives' own strict tribal laws, attempting to impose on them in return a new religion which they did not understand, and to which few white men gave either belief or allegiance.

The huge quantities of whiskey which came into the country forced the government to send in an army of police to ensure that liquor wasn't sold to the Natives, at least not openly. Natives managed to get enough of it to cause death and dishonour to many of their own people; they were punished for crimes committed while they were in delirium from the new "firewater," while the suppliers went free.

Native people of North America were once great people, and they will be again, not because of white "civilization," but in spite of it.

CHAPTER SEVEN

Much
Ado
About
a Dress

"EVE! WHERE IN THE WORLD ARE YOU?" Dan called to me again.

"Here I am," I answered in a much-muffled voice, "under the bed."

"What on earth are you doing there? Come on out, there's nothing to be afraid of!"

"I'm not afraid, I'm just looking for my music. It's in one of these boxes and I moved every one of them before finding it. Here I come!"

Dan laughed immoderately at the spectacle of me crawling backwards from under the bed. He caught me by the ankles, pulled me clear, then helped me to my feet. "You really are a terrible sight." His laughter didn't help me to regain my composure. I was black with dust that had accumulated since the last time I had swept under the bed, for even a good housekeeper wouldn't have moved all those boxes every time she swept, and I wasn't a very good house-keeper. I picked up the box with which I had been wrestling and placed it on a chair.

"Never again will I go through that tunnel to look for anything. The next time we want something out of a box, you can get it and see if you think that's so funny!" Dan stopped laughing.

"Sorry dear, but you did look so comical," he said, and started chuckling again. This time my feelings were really hurt and I walked stiffly past him into the kitchen and washbasin end of the tent. There I washed the dirt off my face and hands, and removed my house dress, which was the dirtiest of all.

Dan said contritely, "I'm sorry I laughed at you, because I really wanted to ask a favour of you."

"What do you want me to do? Feed another dozen of your strays?" I was still sulking, but his reply snapped me out of it quickly.

"No, I just wondered if you could do something about arranging a concert or entertainment of some kind in the church. The summer is over, the days are growing shorter, and I think the folks would like it. What do you think?"

My grievance was forgotten in a moment, and we began at once to plan a Thanksgiving celebration. We felt there must be plenty of talent in the town if we could just find it, so the following Sunday, Dan announced from the pulpit that anyone who might help with a concert should wait until after the service to discuss the feasibility of such an event.

In less than a week we had more offers to perform than we had expected, among them voices for a mixed quartet, which would begin to rehearse immediately; a young man who recited in dialect; a banjo player; a baritone, and a tenor. The baritone was a well-known young man, Scotty Olgivie, who worked on the telegraph line. Tragically, he was drowned years later, in a river which flowed by his cabin, many miles north of Hazelton. There was also a lady who approached me and said shyly, "I'm Mrs. Devlin now, but before I was married, I was a singer in the dance hall in Dawson City. They called me Dolly Louise, and such a favourite I was with my singing, my dear!"

"Then you will sing for us at the concert?"

She agreed enthusiastically. "I would love to sing if you will play for me. I want to practice a bit as I haven't sung for years, and my voice is a bit rusty." My enthusiasm dimmed slightly, but I agreed to play for her.

When the evening of the concert arrived, I was extremely nervous, in part because I would have to attend the affair alone. Dan had been called several miles down the river where a team of horses had been injured in an accident. With fear and trembling I had promised to go early and greet everyone in his name.

The church hall was the upper floor of a large frame building which had several shops below. It was directly across the street from the Ingenika Hotel.

Most of the miners and prospectors were in from their claims for the winter, and the trappers were still waiting for snow to go out to their lines. The Natives' dogs swarmed everywhere, hungry and unpredictably dangerous when they got together in packs.

Walking down the sloping street toward the town, I found myself right in the middle of what looked to my unhappy eyes like a pack of ferocious wolves. I am not afraid of dogs ordinarily, but these almost feral huskies had me trembling with fear. They blocked the narrow sidewalk completely and I had to take to the road. Just as I reached it, they surged in front of me. By this time, my knees were giving way as I headed back to the sidewalk. Then a man's voice called to me from a nearby window, "Pick up that stick there beside you, and if they come again jest lay inta them. They're scared of a stick." I was glad to hear that they, too, could be afraid of something.

"Thanks very much, I'll try it!" I said, picking up the stick. By this time, to my delight, the dogs had moved back until they were behind me and I was free. I dared not run for fear they would chase me, but I walked as quickly as I could and was away from them in a few seconds.

But I still had to pass the hotel. There were at least fifty men milling around outside the door and on the sidewalk, most of them in some stage of mild intoxication. Just as I was deciding to cross the road again, the crowd parted and one old miner bowed low and doffed his hat. "We won't hurt you, little lady," he said. "We're jes' a little drunk, but we never bother a lady."

A giant of a man who came lurching out of the hotel just then must have thought the miner was obstructing my path. He staggered up to him and swept him back with a powerful swing of his arm, saying emphatically, "Leave li'l lady alone, you drunken bum! Mus'n bother her! Know who she is? She's Mrs. Doc and he's an awful big feller. He could tear you apart, an' eat you all up!" Then he stood back, hat held to his breast, his shoulders squared as if daring anyone to even speak to me.

By this time I was laughing hysterically, and, waving my hand at my well-meaning but intoxicated protectors, I hurried across the street and entered the doorway leading upstairs. I ran up the stairway and dropped exhausted into the nearest seat. There was no one else in the hall as yet, so I was able to get myself under control before the crowd arrived.

I was to learn during my stay in the North that I was no safer in my tent under my husband's care than I was on that crowded street. One unpleasant word uttered, one movement toward me, and the offender would have been punished on the spot. In fact, I soon felt safer among these men of the far land, in whatever condition they might be, than I sometimes had been on the streets of my home town, back east.

When the audience began arriving, the hall soon filled, all seats were occupied, and many spectators were forced to stand along the walls. The concert began and was received with vigorous applause. Then Mrs. Devlin's solo was announced. For some reason, we had not been able to get together to practice, so when she gave me her music I was relieved to see it was a simple song which shouldn't be too difficult to accompany, if she was familiar with it. After the first notes I wasn't sure. She may have been a fairly good singer when she was Dolly Louise, but time had not been kind. Her voice was powerful but scarcely sweet, and she couldn't stay in the same key for two lines at a time. I chased her up and down the keyboard for three verses of "'Twas Just a Humble Cottage," and I could see the audience struggling with its laughter. Mrs. Devlin's voice faltered more than once, and her hands were trembling, but she kept her chin high and sang through to the end.

Her courage seemed to impress the audience, and when she finished her song she was given an enthusiastic round of applause. When she said goodnight to me, and thanked me for playing her accompaniment, I hoped she could read in my eyes the sympathy I felt, as plainly as I could see the pain in hers.

Two days later Dan returned from the freight camp and found me in tears, whether of sorrow or rage I wasn't sure. He asked what was wrong, and I told him, "That old busybody, Mrs. McLuckie was just here and said she didn't think the dress I wore at the concert was quite in keeping with my position as a minister's wife. What do you think of that? Do I look like a hussy?"

"I wish I had been here!"

"She probably wouldn't have said a word about it if you had been. Vultures only attack helpless things."

"Now, before I admit you are a helpless thing I'll have to hear what you told her. You're usually able to hold your own."

I just sat there and cried miserably. "I didn't say a word, I couldn't! I was so surprised and hurt. I can't imagine what was wrong with my dress. Others liked it."

The dress in question was part of my trousseau, my one and only party dress. It was of black satin with a narrow hobble skirt down to my ankles. It was made with a modest neckline and fitted snugly over my hips in princess style, with a short overskirt of chiffon. I thought it was lovely, but Mrs. McLuckie thought it improper as she explained, patiently, "You know, my dear, it was quite noticeable and you should be like Caesar's wife, above suspicion."

What she suspected me of I couldn't imagine.

Just then Marie tapped at the door and came in. When she heard my story she laughed and said, "Please, please, don't worry about her, she's just jealous! She couldn't wear a dress like that, she'd look like a scarecrow. You mustn't let little things worry you, or you'll never survive."

Between them, Dan and Marie managed to comfort me and I sat up and dried my tears. A few days later something happened which made me understand to some degree what Mrs. McLuckie meant. The wife of the government agent invited me to a tea, which was the first social event of the season. Of course, I wanted to look my best, so I wore my wedding suit which had a moderate hobble skirt; on my head was a hat with plumes. I hoped this outfit would meet with Mrs. McLuckie's approval. Indeed, I was quite proud of my appearance, especially as I thought my outfit likely to be smarter than those of the other guests.

As I walked past the police station I saw the police chief standing in the door way talking to one of the engineers from the railway camp. Just ahead of me were two prostitutes from the "two-mile" village; another strolled along not far behind. When I was opposite the two men, I heard the engineer say, without lowering his voice in the least, "Nice get-up, that snappy skirt and the hat with plumes! By Jove! She must be a new one. Thought I knew them all. When did she arrive?"

By this time the police chief had recognized me and had come to attention sharply. Even in my acute embarrassment, I couldn't help being amused at the look on his face as he unceremoniously pulled the engineer back through the doorway and said, "You damned idiot! That's the new parson's wife!"

My smile was fast turning to tears when I noticed the two women who had been in front of me. They weren't laughing, and one of them was Lily, whose little dog had died. She said gently, "We're awfully sorry, Mrs. MacLean, but please don't mind too much. It was intended as a compliment, I think, because we always try to dress like ladies, even if we aren't."

I smiled faintly as I thanked her, and went on down the street. As soon as I arrived home, I tore the plumes off my hat and put them in the bottom of my trunk where they remained for years.

The incident enabled me to understand what Mrs. McLuckie had meant when she had spoken to me about my party dress. I learned, too, that the women whose occupation I despised possessed humour and sympathy, and that even the dress of a respectable housewife could give a wrong impression.

I was surprised to find in this new country that the women who were prostitutes were treated like human beings; while the town's women did not like them, they treated them civilly when they came in contact with them in the town. In my old home, prostitutes were looked upon as pariahs, and they were forced to always keep out of the sight of the general public. For a respectable woman to be seen speaking to a known professional would have been considered scandalous. I found the professional prostitutes in the North much preferable to the hypocritical amateurs I met during my years in the city.

CHAPTER EIGHT

A Sick Pony,
a Bad Deal,
and
a Secret

As soon as it became known that there was a veterinary surgeon in town the Natives began to wear a path to our door. Their ponies were thin and looked half-starved, and many had sores on their shoulders caused by loose packsaddles which had rubbed their hides raw.

One evening, just at dusk, I heard a noisy commotion outside the tent and looked out. Several Natives were there, all talking at once and gesticulating towards me. One of them asked, "Where horse-doctor man?"

"Down in the village just now, but he'll be back soon," (I hoped). But the man wasn't satisfied and, brushing past me, he stalked into the tent and looked all around until he was sure I was telling the truth. Then he broke into a torrent of words, both Native and English, supplementing words with signs and gestures until I gathered that his pony had tried to jump a picket fence with disastrous results.

"Guts all out through hole. Doctor man put 'em back and fasten up hole," he said. It sounded quite a job, even for Dan.

Just when I began to think they intended to make me do the job myself, Dan walked in. I explained what the trouble was, but the Native was pacified only when Dan picked up his surgical bag and a kettle of hot water and started for the door. I trailed behind the procession with an armful of bandages and a pan of instruments to the field where the poor animal lay moaning with pain. There was a hole in the pony's belly and various loops and bulges had escaped its confines. The job looked messy and difficult, but Dan went to work at once.

No chloroform was available and the drug store was closed for the night, so the pony had to be trussed up with rope and the Natives persuaded to hold him still. The pony's owner poured the kettle of hot water over my pan of instruments, while one of the others held the bandages. All went well as Dan sterilized the affected area, and returned the animal's intestines to its abdominal cavity, then he prepared to sew up the wound. The pony's owner took one long, agonized look at the big curved needle, dropped the kettle, and fled into the night, accompanied by another man who pushed the bandages into my already full arms. It was fortunate that the Natives who held the pony down stayed with their job.

When the operation was completed, Dan stood admiring his handiwork for a moment, saying, "That's as pretty a piece of embroidery as I've ever done."

The pony was placed in a blanket sling under a sheltering shed roof nearby with his feet dangling a few inches off the ground. The Natives vied with each other in attending to the poor beast, keeping him fed and watered and exhibiting the "embroidery" to everybody who came along.

Considering that the wound had been stuffed with dirty gunny sacks when Dan came onto the scene and blood poisoning had seemed inevitable, the operation was successful. When the pony had recovered and was walking around once more, the Natives came in ever increasing numbers, leading sick ponies and mangy dogs for treatment. Sometimes I wished the gunny sacks had been more potent, but Dan was too keenly interested in healing sick animals to turn any of them away.

The Natives were skeptical of the white men's methods, with good reason, and would not pay for any medical work until the animal was cured. Then they were very grateful and would bring a load of wood, a sack of potatoes, a nice fresh salmon or well-woven basket, which was received with thanks.

But their dogs really exasperated us. We had been warned that they became very hungry as winter approached and the supply of smoked salmon was rationed, but we didn't know they could tear their way through one-inch-thick boards to get at a meat safe. We had to put our meat box up high on a pole to save our ham and bacon.

One pack of dogs dug and chewed their way through the floor of the Hudson's Bay warehouse, and by the time the hole was discovered they had devoured dozens of cans of fish and meat. The huskies would take a can between their forepaws and cut the lid out neatly with their sharp fangs, swallowing the contents in one gulp. To us, this seemed like poetic justice, as the dogs would have to eat a mountain of Hudson's Bay Company food before the Natives could be compensated for the amounts stolen from them by traders.

The dogs liked live chickens too, and anyone who kept a few for table use had to guard them very carefully. Mr. Smith, owner of a small store near us, kept a pen of purebred chickens in his yard and a loaded gun at the back door, ready for use at the slightest squawk from the back yard. One day, after hearing terrified squawking, he dashed outside just in time to see a gaunt, hungry husky about to devour a hen. Mr. Smith shot the dog before he had time to get a single mouthful. Almost at once, a Native appeared demanding payment for "one good sled dog."

"I tell Indian Agent and he make you pay me for shoot my dog!"

"But look here, Amos, you see my dead hen? Your dog killed my hen, so I killed your dog."

"I know you shoot him, I see! You pay me now!"

"No, I won't pay you Amos, but I'll tell you what we'll do. Your dog came in my yard and killed my hen, right?"

"Yes, I guess he kill him."

"All right then, sometime maybe my hen go in your yard and kill your dog. You shoot my hen, then we be even. That's fair, eh?"

The Native scratched his head for a moment, then nodded, "Yah, that all right. Sometime maybe I kill your hen."

The Native went on his way feeling that he received a fair deal, which he had, according to tribal laws. Justice and fair trade had been the Natives' way until white men taught them greed for money and the things it could buy.

Harry Davies was visiting us that evening and we told him about Smith and the Native's deal. He nodded his head, laughing, and said, "Smith is a good sort and treats the Natives fairly enough, much better than most white men in the country. The older Natives are badly worried about the way the younger Natives pick up all the bad habits of the whites, and very few of the good ones. Whiskey! That's the Natives' damnation!"

Lighting his pipe, he continued, "Very well do white men know what they can get for a bottle of whiskey or rum. Many a choice piece of fur and haunch of venison finds its way to white men for a couple of drinks. Whiskey's sure hell in Native country."

"You're right, Harry," Dan observed, "and still the government allows the liquor dealers to charter the first boats of the season to bring in more whiskey instead of much-needed food for the settlers. Then they have to send in an army of police to see that the Natives don't get it — at least not openly."

"You know Doc, I've seen quite a few killings over a bottle of whiskey. White men bring it, give Natives each a drink or two, then try to make a deal with them for something the white men want, promising more whiskey when the deal is made. Once this is accomplished," he said, "the white men refuse to give up their bottles and there's a fight and maybe one of them gets killed. If Natives die, the police usually decide that they had it coming to them, shaking their heads over 'these wild savages,' and the white men go free. If the white men are killed, Natives are hanged."

"Don't the missionaries help the Natives?" asked Dan, "after all that's their job."

"Not at all. The missionaries have been here for a good many years, and there certainly hasn't been much improvement in the lot of the Natives, that I can see. The only thing the missionaries seem interested in is to take the old tribal laws away from them and give them a new religion,which they can't understand; only fear of the unknown god makes them listen. They certainly can't see that white men are any the better for going to the church."

"Are they all like that, the missionaries, I mean?"

"No, some of them are pretty good men, but they are sadly out-numbered. It's puzzling to the Native mind, though, and makes them suspicious of the white man's god. One old Native was arrested for stealing some wire from the trading post. The missionary here — one of the best he was — went to see the Native who was part of his flock. He asked him why he did such a thing, after being taught that stealing was wrong. "I've tried to teach you to be honest, so why do you steal?"

"You funny white man! You not like other white men; white men always steal from Natives, so Native steal from white man!"

"And that just about sums up the matter," said Harry. "The missionaries are white men too, and the Natives don't understand the differences in their behaviours."

For a moment he sat silent and a little smile played about his lips. "The missionaries have certainly made things easier for the white traders, taming the Natives with all their talk about hell fire for those who do not believe their teachings. The old tribal laws, the Natives' religion, were good laws," he said. "When the occasional renegade breaks the tribe's law, his chief punishes him. Usually a bad Native is banished from the tribe. In communal living such as theirs, this is almost equal to death, and is pretty effective punishment," he said. "It's hard for them to understand why bad white men are allowed to stay in the community, much less become leaders as they sometimes do."

As the conversation continued over coffee and biscuits, my husband said, "I'm sure you're right Harry, but nonetheless it's not good to hear. There must be some good white men."

"There are, Doc, there are! It's not the individual man I mean, but the institutions, the big traders, the government and the church. To them," he said, "the Indians are not people, just howling savages, and, I regret to say, many of us take on the colour of our leaders. Even in the church you know, the old saying is true, 'The man who pays the piper calls the tune.'"

"That's true," my husband agreed. "I know because I've had a little experience along that line and I don't like it."

"Well, my friend, when you haven't been to church for many a day, like

75

me, and lived out among men of all sorts, you see things differently. Being a church man doesn't always mean being a good man, and being an unbeliever doesn't necessarily mean being a bad one."

"Just what I have been thinking for a long time, Mr. Davies," I said, laughing as I walked over to the old man, "so shake hands with a heretic!"

Dan chuckled. "Seems to me most of my friends up here are outside the pale from the church's standpoint."

As Harry talked, I was busy remembering something which had happened several years before at home in Ontario.

In one office where I worked I heard much talk of a certain tract about fifty miles down the river which was rich in minerals. The engineers who were making a survey of the property reported that much of the richest part ran across a Native reservation. Something had to be done to obtain the land, and I learned about the shocking transaction in the course of my work. The principal perpetrator was a respected local citizen, treasurer of one of the churches; his partners were two of my company's executives. The local man had been sent to make the deal because he was so well-known and considered to be an honest man. The purchase was made, it seemed, with two bottles of whiskey, consumed on the spot, and twenty dollars for several acres of the richest land in the whole country.

The partners were jubilant when their collaborator returned to the office, waving a paper which had sealed the deal, and they went to work at once to develop the mines, making a great deal of money in the following years.

The more I thought about this matter, the more I realized that white men treated Natives with great similarity whether in the "near land" or the "far land."

"How about some more coffee?" I suggested, hoping to lighten the atmosphere a little. The men agreed enthusiastically.

Dan asked Harry what the Natives thought of the railway. "They don't like it — at least the older ones don't." They had become accustomed to the steamboats after a while," he said, "but one old chief had recently remarked, 'Steamboat come up river, good. Bad water for canoe. Steamboat come up through forest, not good. I not like. We will go.' And away they went," Harry said, "about forty miles north into the wilderness and a new hunting ground."

I wonder what the chief thought when the steamboats began sailing through the air over their heads. They would have to go to the happy hunting ground to get away from them.

The summer days were ended, the daylight hours shorter, and there was a hint of frost in the air. The sheet iron heater we had installed in the centre of the tent was becoming hotter and more of a comfort. How we were able to move around, cook, eat, sleep and entertain our friends in such small quarters I don't know. But we did it, and we were snug and comfortable most of the time, although I confess I wasn't too comfortable some of the time, particularly in the early mornings. One morning, I was curled up on the couch weeping with loneliness and fright when a tap at the door made me sit up suddenly. I expected to see one of my neighbours who had begun to make it her business to come in nearly every morning to see me on some excuse or another. She was determined to be the first to detect signs of pregnancy in the bride. "Come in," I called, and to my great relief it was Marie.

I went to meet her as she closed the door. She looked at me, not curiously but kindly, and said, "What's wrong, Mrs. MacLean? You do look sick! Can I help you?"

"I'm not quite sure, Marie, but I think I'm going to have a baby."

"Why, you lucky gal! Wish I was! Come over here and lie down this minute. Have you had any breakfast?"

"I had my breakfast, but I haven't it now."

"Well, you're going to have another one immediately because you'll starve otherwise."

I stretched out on the couch again while Marie built up the fire, and I was almost asleep when she stood beside me with a breakfast tray. There was a steaming cup of tea, thin bread and butter, and orange marmalade, all on my nicest china dishes.

"Thanks, Marie, that was the best meal I have eaten for a week."

"After this, my dear, you get your husband to give you a cup of coffee and some breakfast in bed," she said, "and don't get up for at least a half hour afterwards. Then you'll keep it down and won't get yourself so badly run down."

I couldn't help wondering how Marie knew so many things that I didn't know about having a baby. Timidly I asked her. She was silent for several minutes and I was afraid I had annoyed her, but she smiled and answered, "Yes, I had a baby once. It died. Or at least, that is what they told me. Since then, I have learned that my little girl was adopted by some people in Seattle. Oh, it was all quite legal, because when they asked me before she was born if I would give her out for adoption, I was quite frantic with worry and didn't know how I could possibly take care of a baby. So I signed the paper. Afterwards, I tried to tell them I would like to keep her and the doctor and nurse looked at each other and told me she had died. She hadn't, but they were afraid to tell me that she had already been taken away."

"How did you find out she had lived after all, and was adopted?"

"One of the other nurses told me about a year later," she said. "Oh, how I wish she hadn't." Marie covered her face with her hands and tears rolled down her cheeks.

Marie went to work sweeping, dusting and washing the dishes. I protested, but she just smiled and went right on working until everything was in order. Then she sat down beside me, and from her serious face, I knew she had something to tell me.

"I'm going away next week, Mrs. MacLean. Nobody else knows, and I won't tell you where I'm going so you will be able to say you don't know anything about it. I know I can trust you not to tell anyone the things I told you about the baby, because even Hank doesn't know."

"Of course I'll respect your confidence, Marie. But why are you going? Is Hank leaving his job?"

"I think he will when he gets my letter. I wrote him last week and sent the letter up with one of the prospectors. I'm going to open a small café somewhere, and I've asked Hank to come and help me."

"I thought you were very happy here, except for Hank being away so much."

"That's just it. With Hank away I have no one. You and your husband have been most kind and friendly, but it isn't good for you to be my friend. I know, I've heard women talking about it."

"I don't care a hoot what they say, Marie, you've been such a good friend and neighbour to me they can say anything they like. It's only the wives of the construction men who talk like that. The old-timers are all your friends, and the others will be gone when the railway is built."

I felt very angry but Marie patted my hand. "I'm going anyway, because it is lonely with Hank away all the time. And there are several men here whom I knew in the Yukon and they just don't seem to believe I am really married to Hank. It's getting to be a nightmare, so I'm going. But I'll be thinking about you and hoping your baby comes along all right."

She stood up, keeping my hand in hers, but I pulled her down and kissed her good-bye. She ran out of the tent, crying.

I lay still for a long time, thinking. Marie had been so kind, so helpful and understanding. She had discarded her blonde wigs and explained that she had worn them when her own hair had fallen out after a serious illness. Now her hair was growing in quickly and was a dark brown, soft and quite curly. It made her look years younger and softened her face lines.

One day she told me her story. She was an orphan, brought up by foster parents who had not been kind to her. As soon as she could, she left them to earn her own living, working in a factory in San Francisco.

With some other factory women, she had begun to attend a dance hall and she was soon working there as a hostess. When the Yukon gold fields beckoned, several of the women, including Marie, had gone to Dawson City as entertainers. She said the rest of the story wasn't for the ears of a minister's wife, but I knew that whatever it was, Marie was a generous, kindhearted woman who had been kind to me, and had taught me to understand many things.

I laughed aloud when I wondered what Mrs. Elmer Baxter would think if she knew my good friend Marie had been one of those "awful creatures" of the Yukon dance halls. As for the old Scottish minister, he would have been more convinced than ever that here "sin doth abound and Satan lifteth up his head."

If he had known anything about the world outside the cloistered walls of his church, he would have known there were plenty of the sinners in his own town. Some of his more sanctimonious churchgoers could have enlightened him, had they so desired.

CHAPTER NINE

The
Unlikely
Confidante

D AN WAS AWAY FROM HOME MOST OF THE TIME that spring and it was lonely for me, but once the small group of women belonging to our congregation were satisfied that their guesses were correct, and I was pregnant, they flooded me with kindnesses. Their favours were hard to accept at first, because at home in eastern Canada, women who were obviously pregnant usually would not have appeared in public. Babies and their origins were supposedly a profound secret from the younger generation, and children received little or no instruction about sex, other than grotesque information from our schoolmates.

The loneliness persisted, however, because there are so many things I would have liked to discuss, but dared not mention to anyone, least of all a member of the congregation. I wished I had a dog to talk to, because he, at least, would not repeat our conversations.

My best confidante was a mule. He was big and black and a member of one of the packtrains that carried mail and supplies to prospectors and trappers all through the Skeena Valley by way of the mountain trails to the Interior. The packtrain would be loaded up in the Hudson's Bay Company corral and, as each animal received his pack, he waited for the others. But one of them, the big black mule, would leave the corral and follow the road up the hill to the

Hudson's Bay Packtrain. This road passed the tent as it curved away to the right.

enclosure in which we lived. There was a gap in the fence and he used to come in and lie down, carefully, so as not to dislodge his pack. He liked to nibble the green grass within reach, and sometimes, while he ate, I would go out and sit down beside him and pat his big face. Then I would talk to him, since he seemed to be the ideal confidante.

He always rested quietly for perhaps an hour, and then I would see his long ears tip forward, and his head turn as he heard footsteps to which my ears were deaf. Slowly he would rise, walk to the gap in the fence, and as the thudding of many feet became louder, and the train appeared and filed past, he would step into his place in the line, with what I flattered myself was a regretful look. In a few minutes, the packtrain would all be out of sight around the curve of the hill.

The packtrains would travel from ten to fifteen miles a day, walking quickly without resting to the end of the day's march. If the packs were insecurely fastened, they would slip forward on the down hill paths and back again on the upgrade. The result was often painful sores on the animal's shoulders.

The trails led over mountains where the view is something to thrill even the most seasoned traveller; where the torrential rivers in the bed of the valley appear from the hilltop like a fine thread of silver ribbon. A single misstep might mean falling hundreds of feet into the rocky canyon beds, so both men and animals stepped carefully, as even a mule has no desire to be dashed to pieces.

The best part of the journey for the packtrain came when the destination was reached and the eager men pulled the packs from the animals' tired shoulders. With the packtrain came letters from home, food, tobacco, magazines, and parcels to cheer those in lonely places. It was like Christmas and birthdays in one for those men of the mines and traplines.

Well fed and rested, the packtrain returned home to Hazelton, sometimes carrying furs or other, lighter, loads for the market. There was a little grassy spot about a mile from town, beside the Aldermere road, where the packtrains used to stop on the last night out. It was a sheltered spot with plenty of grazing and a small creek. As the tired, dusty and thirsty animals neared this spot they could smell the water, and, in their eagerness to plunge their noses in its clear coolness their lagging steps would hasten and they would break into a run for the last few yards. Packs off, they would roll over and over in the grass, happy to be free again.

The day of the packtrain is over, except in a very few places, but in those early days of the century, and before, it was not only a picturesque sight but a necessity. The long-suffering animals were as truly pioneers as any trapper, prospector, or trader who opened the northern valleys. The animals carried mail to cheer the heart, food to sustain life, and supplies to enable the people in remote outposts to carry on their work. Many a man owes his life, as well as his fortune, to the horses, mules, and dogs of those packtrains.

Later, when roads were built, and freight wagons rolled up and down the valley, followed by railroad trains unloading at every station, the packtrains gradually disbanded. Now planes carry mail, passengers, food, and medical supplies to distant points in a fraction of the time taken then, and it is easy to forget the sturdy mules, the tireless dogs, and patient ponies, but to old northerners, they remain a vivid memory.

Where there were roads, the stagecoaches, too, played an important role in opening the country. They travelled swiftly along the frozen trails and rivers in winter and the rough and rutted roads in summer.

I'll never forget the stagecoach that travelled down the Aldermere road from the eastern part of the valley to Hazelton every week. The driver had a habit of reinforcing himself with a few drinks at each stopping place along the way, so he was usually in a high state of hilarity when he arrived at the top of the hill leading down into Hazelton. There he sat, perched on the high seat, throwing his long whip out over the backs of six running mules, and swaying with every bump in the road. He sang, shouted, and cursed merrily all the way to the stage stop, then, pulling the mules to a running stop, he would jump to the ground with a piercing yell. How he managed to keep that hightopped stage right side up on the steep and crooked hill was a constant wonder to everyone. I don't think he ever had an accident, but that was probably more to the credit of the mules than to his driving.

In late October, the daylight shortened and twilight came earlier, so we were forced to light our lamps at three o'clock in the afternoon. We were sad to see the last boat of the season slip away from the wharf into midstream for it was only a few minutes before the swift current bore the vessel downstream and around the first bend of the river. That was when my heart ached for a sight of Ontario in October, with its autumn colours and rich harvests, and when home did indeed seem far away.

After the riverboats were tied up for the winter, everything seemed to be quiet. At that time there were five riverboats operating all summer long, the *Hazelton* and the *Port Simpson* of the Hudson's Bay Company fleet; the *Inlander*, which was owned by the independent traders, and the Foley, Welch and Stewart boats, the *Conveyor* and the *Distributor*. Now we received only letter mail from the coast, carried by dog sled up the trail which followed the river, frozen and silent. The long twilight was upon us and we were in a world of our own. There was no other place.

CHAPTER TEN

Of Dogs
and
Dog Men

Through the long summer days, the sun shone brightly until the evening faded into twilight an hour or so before midnight, and it wasn't much use to try to sleep before that time. It was shining again about three o'clock in the morning and, the tent being small protection against daylight, we found it hard to get sufficient rest. We were looking forward to the long dark nights of winter when we would be able to catch up on our sleep. But we reckoned without the dogs!

It was impossible to overlook the numerous dogs in Hazelton. Almost everyone, whites and Natives, had a string of sled dogs, and the pups were of every size and description. Howling huskies! Hundreds of them! In the daytime they swarmed into the streets of the town, parading up and down like fraternal societies, and at night they howled. If the moon appeared they serenaded it for hours, beginning around midnight, or as soon as we were comfortably asleep. One howl sounded from the riverbank, one from higher up, then one or two from the top of the hill behind us; back to the river level again, with perhaps a dozen or more joining in all at once, back and forth, up and down, in the manner of a Bach fugue, until the air was filled with sound, and the night made hideous with the mournful wailing.

We could no more shut out the sound with blankets over our heads than we used to be able to ignore Ontario lightning. Not until the dogs had tired of their nocturnal serenade were we able to compose ourselves to sleep, heads aching and vocabularies exhausted.

The log cabin next door had some new occupants. The McKay boys had gone down to the coast for a holiday and three or four prospectors had come to live in the cabin. Harry Davies, who had been fairly successful in his prospecting years, had retired, and moved into a cabin nearby. Since he was in his late seventies, it was time he took a rest from labour.

The new neighbours had moved in after dark one evening, and since we had not seen them, we did not know they were there. I discovered their presence the next morning when I went outside to draw a pail of water from the well. To my amazement, I found myself facing six large and ferocious wolves, or so I thought at the time.

It was my first introduction to a really splendid wolf-dog sled team, and there and then I proved the old adage that fools rush in where sane people stay out. The owner of the team told me afterwards, "God certainly protects fools and children, and you ain't no child!" Five of these magnificent animals were malamutes, large, powerful and heavy-footed, and all had coats of varying shades of grey. The sixth was a proud golden sable collie. He stood closest to me, his ruff bristling, his teeth bared.

I love dogs, and don't fear them, and I can usually make friends with any kind of dog. This time, however, I was frightened nearly to death, although I determined not to let them find it out. Really my surprise and admiration nearly eliminated my fear. The collie looked more familiar than the others so I concentrated on him, holding out my hands and saying softly, "Hello there, you beautiful thing! Where in the world did you come from? Come here and talk to me, don't be afraid, I just want to be friends," and so on, over and over.

At first I thought he was going to ignore my chatter, but the tone of my voice must have reassured him, for he stopped snarling and his shoulder hair subsided. Inch by inch he crept forward as I continued my monologue, and then he was sniffing my fingers. A blue-grey husky, looking exactly like a timber wolf, took a step toward me. My feet were glued to the ground and my voice took on a husky tone. I swallowed a couple of times to keep my heart down where it belonged. As the blue husky stood beside the collie, watching my fingers gently stroking the slender golden muzzle, while the other four stood in a circle with heads lowered and their wicked eyes staring at me, a man stepped through the doorway of the cabin. With a horrified gasp he dashed back into the cabin to return immediately with a big dishpan on which he beat a tattoo with a stick.

The dogs ran to him at once at the sound of their dinner bell, and the prospector threw some smoked salmon at their feet. Then he came toward me and said, coldly, "Sorry to break up the party, ma'am, but those dogs would have torn you to pieces in another minute." Then more sharply, "Didn't you know that was a silly thing to do, to stand there talking to a bunch of wild malamutes? Those dogs have never seen a white woman before, let alone been touched by one!"

"Is that really so? That's their loss. They may be fierce but they're more polite than you are!" I replied tartly. "How was I supposed to get to the well without running into them?"

The prospector, whose name, I learned, was Andy Chase, blushed. "My goodness, ma'am, we didn't know there was a woman in that tent, we just got in from the hills last night. Anyhow, a man would have had more sense than to talk to strange dogs like that."

I could laugh about it now that I was safe. "Do you really think I was in danger? You interrupted me just when I was about to convince them they could learn to love me. I bet I could make friends with every one of them. How long will they be around?

"We're in for the winter. Been out prospecting all summer."

"All right. I'll have those dogs eating out of my hand in two weeks, and if I don't, I'll make you a big, juicy pie. Is it a bet?

"Think you can, ma'am?" Then more scornfully, "them dogs is mostly wolf, except the Pup and he won't let anyone but me put a hand . . . ." At that point, his voice faded and his eyes nearly popped out of his head. Pup was gently licking my fingers. I smiled smugly.

It took me slightly less than the two weeks to make friends with them, because when the malamutes saw me feeding the collie, whose name was Pup, they decided to get in on the free lunch. They also found out that I loved all animals and that I was not afraid of them. Andy said it was "nothin' but cupboard love," but when he saw his savage wolves come running to meet me and letting me pet them, he lost his bet. To compensate for Andy's embarrassment, I invited him and his partner to supper one evening, and made two raisin pies, one for the table and one for them to take home, and they told me to go ahead and tame their dogs as much as I liked. They complained however, that I had made their good sled dogs into lap dogs, and they hadn't had a fight for a week, except when Old Blue, the biggest one, turned on Pup through jealousy. But I heard later they had been boasting around town about how I had tamed their team.

Shortly after this we acquired a team of our own. It was the only way to travel for any distance, except by horseback, and we had no horses. The team consisted of four dogs. Wolf was the leader, a cross between a collie and a setter, and possibly one or more other breeds. Nick was a golden dog, part Saint Bernard, which made him nearly as big as a bear, and Teddy was seven-eighths wolf. Last but not least was Bildad, an Eskimo husky.

Bildad adopted us as his foster parents when he was not quite full-grown, hungry, mangy, and apparently lost. We took him in and Dan cured his mange, then started to train him as a sled dog. He looked like an overgrown Spitz, reddish tan in colour and his eyes were very much like those of a pig. Not a beautiful dog, by any means, but he was very strong, although lazy. Why Dan named him Bildad I couldn't understand, but he said the dog reminded him somewhat of a certain Bildad in the Bible.

Bildad behaved himself very well, and in a few weeks he learned to work a little harder. Then, one morning he was gone. Dan went all around the reserve looking for him and finally found him tied outside a Native's cabin. His harness lay on the ground beside him. The Native said, "This is my dog. When he was a pup he come to your house and you feed him. All right, you feed him if you like, but now I need him. If you take him away, I go to Indian Agent and he make you pay twenty-five dollars for one good sled dog, and if you no pay, I say you steal him!"

And that was that! However, Dan took the harness since the Native could not claim it. And should anyone think that the Native was being unreasonable, that person should see the way the white men stole their dogs from the Natives!

We tried to replace Bildad with one of Teddy's brothers, but like some human relatives, they did not get along well and they fought every time they found themselves in harness.

Nick was such a splendid dog that we often brought him into the tent, though he took up a good deal of space in such tightly crowded quarters. But that privilege was denied him for the rest of his life after what happened one night just before Christmas.

We had loaned our team to a YMCA social worker, Big Bill Morrison, and he brought them back one snowy evening just at suppertime. I had supper all ready for Dan and two of the inevitable guests, when the door flew open, in bounded Big Bill, and close beside him, Nick, both of them covered with snow.

Big Bill shouted, "Supper ready, Mrs. Doc? How about some hot biscuits, I'm hungrier than a houn' dawg!"

I started immediately to make the biscuits, as Bill had an appetite to tax the ingenuity of a cook in that land without bakeries. In record time I was taking a pan of biscuits from the oven of my little sheet iron stove.

The tent, which was full before, was overflowing. Bill was six feet one, and weighed 230 pounds. Dan was six-three, and weighed 210 pounds. Fortunately, the others were small men, and I kept out of the way as much as possible. Besides all the furniture and people, Nick, the Saint Bernard, was stretched out enjoying the warmth and rest, right across the doorway between the kitchen end of the tent and the supper table.

I piled the pan full of biscuits on one of my wedding presents, a blue willow pattern platter, and started for the table. Just as I stepped over the apparently sleeping dog, he sprang to his feet, and I went sprawling. There were biscuits flying in every direction while I lay on my back on the floor holding aloft half a broken plate.

I rose to a sitting position, looking so sad and helpless that the four men were roaring with laughter as they scrambled around trying to retrieve the biscuits. Nick ate four or five before they threw him outside, and I rose to my feet quite unassisted. I wasn't laughing, I was furious! With icy dignity, I told the still laughing men I wouldn't make any more biscuits if they starved to death. "And, what's more, in future that dog will stay outside!"

Right then I felt eager and willing to live the rest of my life without the sight of another man or dog.

CHAPTER ELEVEN

Our
First
Christmas

I WAS TAUGHT IN MY CHILDHOOD that any man who looked upon the wine when it was red, was already a lost soul. My father and mother were opposed to liquor in any form, so of course, I had always agreed with them. They were almost as much opposed to the use of tobacco.

One old country Scottish minister who boarded with us for a year, loved to smoke a pipe after dinner, and at bedtime. He was forced to take a walk in the woods for his after-dinner smoke, and to wait until we were all in bed to open his window and smoke beside it, no matter how cold it was. The next morning when my mother was making his bed, she would sometimes sniff the air and say, "That man has been smoking in here!"

Later, as I grew up, my experience taught me that some very nice people smoked tobacco and even drank liquor in moderation, so I worried no longer about those two particular sins. I also learned slowly that people should not be judged by appearances only, that there was no such thing as all good, or all bad, and that the people we found most congenial and friendly were a comfortable shade of grey.

In the North, beyond the pale of civilization as we had known it, we met former millionaires, former bankers and business men, men of all professions from the four corners of the earth. There were men who were trying to forget past failures or find new fortunes in a new country. There were wife-deserters, actors, gamblers and adventurers, members of long-scattered gangs of bandits who had achieved international fame. But most of them were true pioneers or sons of pioneers, who had come to build and not destroy. It was sometimes necessary to make a quick reversal in an opinion made without knowledge of its subject. Gradually, my stiff-necked Presbyterian convictions abated for living close to nature, whether animate or inanimate, outer appearances don't mean so much. The artificialities of life have a way of peeling off, leaving only the truth, or part of the truth.

In a small shack on the edge of town, there lived a man some people might call a derelict. He certainly looked like one. He loved two things, his horse and whiskey. I had never seen him at close range until one day when he came to our door and asked in a desperate voice, "For God's sake, Doc, will you come down and look at my little mare, Dolly. She's groaning and sweating and trembling like she had a chill.

"Of course, Jimmie, right away. Sounds like pneumonia, and if it is, there's no time to lose. Come on!"

"God bless you, Doc! I haven't much, but if you save Dolly for me, anything I have is yours!" With that, the two men hurried off to the barn where the sick Dolly was kept.

It took three days of careful nursing and strenuous dosing before Dolly began to recover, but a week later she was herself again. Jimmie was tearfully grateful and told Doc, "There isn't anything you can ask me, Doc, that I wouldn't do for you. Dolly is the best friend I've ever had, almost the only one I have now, and you've saved her for me."

"I'm glad I was able to save her, Jimmie. I don't like to see any animal suffer, and she's a fine little mare. Yes, there's one thing you could do, Jimmie, you can come up and have supper with us tomorrow night, and we'll have a chat. Might get better acquainted."

Jimmie looked quite stricken for a minute, then he laughed, "I said I'd do anything, didn't I Doc? Well, I'll do it. Six o'clock all right?"

Dan nodded, "See you then, Jimmie, and don't forget!"

The next evening there was a firm knock at the door and I opened it. There stood a complete stranger, until I noticed a merry twinkle in his eyes, and recognized Jimmie. Gone were the whiskers, the soiled, untidy clothing, the bleary eyes and unsteady feet. In their place stood a pleasant-looking young man, perfectly sober and clean shaven, and dressed in a dark grey suit, clean shirt, and blue tie. In his hand was a hat, obviously new, and conservative in style. He was laughing now at my astonished face, as I almost whispered, "Come in." He entered and shook hands with Dan, who looked almost as bewildered as I did.

Before sitting down, Jimmie walked immediately to the bookcase. He stood, feasting his eyes on the books, as though greeting old friends. He and Dan talked of this writer and that, of poets, philosophers and historians, and as he talked Jimmie's hands stroked lovingly the bindings of the books. He opened one of them so eagerly that Dan asked him, "Have you read that one, Jimmie?"

"Not the translation, I've only read it in the original. Could I possibly, I mean, would you let me have it for a few days?"

"Certainly, certainly, take anything you see that interests you!" Dan was delighted to find a fellow book lover, especially one who could read volumes in their original Greek. Jimmie was standing quite still, with rather a lost look on his face. Then he said, quietly, "I have never told anyone this before out here, Doc, but I received my Master's degree from McGill University in 1902. Please don't mention it to anyone, they wouldn't believe it anyway. Since then I have become a drunken fool, interested only in destroying myself. Right now, I feel terribly ashamed. Tomorrow I shall probably be very drunk, again."

"Why, Jimmie? Why did you throw yourself away like that? There aren't enough men of education, and I'm sure you could have made a good place for yourself in this new country. What profession were you entering?"

"Law! What a lawyer I would have been! No, Doc, I'm afraid I'm an alcoholic. It ruined me in the East."

"Could you tell me about it, Jimmie? Sometimes it does one good to talk."

"Might as well, I guess, now that you know this much. I was a hockey player throughout my high school years, and in university. Pretty good, they told me, too. When I was ready to enter the law school, I was playing with a senior hockey team, in Montreal. Playing and studying at the same time was quite a grind, and I began to drink a little to bolster up my ambition. Then I was offered a place on the professional team. I played for most of one season, but by this time I was drinking more and more, and one night I went on the ice slightly intoxicated. The coach warned me, but I just laughed and said I was quite all right. I wasn't. I not only lost them the game by my antics, but was suspended for the rest of the season. On the way home that night, I had a few more drinks and when a friendly chap, one of my teammates, met me, he tried to get me to go home and sleep it off. I struck him and he fell, striking his head against a hydrant. He almost died."

"When I was certain he would recover," he continued," I left the city and came out here, thinking I would get a fresh start and maybe stop drinking. What a hope! You can see for yourself the kind of start I made."

"Jimmie, don't you think you could stop drinking and take up where you left off?" Dan asked. "You're a young man, and it would take a lot of courage, but I'm sure you could do it if you tried. I'd like to help you."

"Don't waste your time on me, Doc. I have no courage left, and please let's not talk about it anymore. I see Mrs. MacLean is waiting for us to come to supper. Thanks a lot, Doc."

The rest of the evening passed pleasantly, talking about hockey, horses, and the north, and when he was leaving, Jimmie thanked me warmly for the supper and our hospitality. With a rather crooked smile he said, "You're a brave woman, Mrs. MacLean. No other woman in town would have risked an invitation to supper for fear I would accept."

My face was very red. I, too, had been more than a little disturbed when Dan told me he had asked Jimmie to come that evening. But I had not finished learning about people in this strange and wonderful country, and several lessons awaited me.

It would be my first Christmas away from home and I wasn't looking forward to it with much pleasure. Christmas at home had always been such a happy occasion and I felt very far away and lonely. Dan's home had been different. His father was away at sea most of the time and his mother died when he was just a boy, so Christmas hadn't meant quite so much to him. I was determined to see that he enjoyed this one, and I hid my loneliness as much as possible as the season approached. The problem was solved one day when Dan said, "Eve, what would you say to going down river to the bridge camp for Christmas?"

"I think it would be fun, but what would we do down there?"

"Big Bill is having a Christmas party for the men that night, and he wants us to go down. He has a little portable organ, and he wants you to sing and play for them, and I'm to give them a short talk. I think we should try to go and help Bill. We're invited to have our Christmas dinner there."

"Christmas dinner in a construction camp! What do you suppose we'd get to eat?"

"Look," he explained patiently, "the bridge camp has the best cook on construction, and they have all the food necessary for any emergency. We'll get plenty of dinner."

"All right, then, I'm all for it. It'll be a change from bacon and eggs, anyway, and a rest for me. But we couldn't come back that night, we'd have to sleep there."

"Don't worry," Dan laughed, "you won't have to sleep in the bunk house. There's one woman in camp, Mrs. Marsden, the wife of one of the engineers. They live in a tent and she said she would take care of you and send her husband to the bunkhouse with me."

So all the arrangements were made for our trip. We left about three in the afternoon of Christmas Day when they sent a team of horses and a sleigh for us. They would get us down to the camp in time for supper.

The snow was falling in large, soft flakes from a sky dark with clouds, not a breath of wind was stirring in the trees which lined the road that followed the winding course of the river.

We sat on a pile of straw in the back of the sleigh, well wrapped in blankets. The horse bells and our own voices were the only sounds to be heard. The horses' hooves and the runners of the sleigh were alike noiseless. Not a rustle broke the deep silence, the perfect quiet filled with peace on earth.

We arrived at the camp just in time to enjoy a staggering meal. George, the cook, had certainly done himself proud with this Christmas dinner. Though he did not have turkey, there was prime roast beef, roast pork, roast potatoes and several varieties of vegetables and pickles. There was a Christmas pudding, mince pie, apple pie, cookies, and doughnuts. We ate so much we were forced to excuse ourselves by saying the long drive had made us very hungry. Immediately after the meal, we went over to the recreation hall and the crowds of men waiting for their entertainment. There must have been at least 350 of them, of almost every nationality. After serious talks by Bill and Dan, we settled down to enjoy ourselves in more informal fashion. Pails of candy and boxes of oranges were passed around, and I seated myself at the organ to sing and play for them. For nearly two hours I pumped that miserable little excuse for an organ and sang song after song, the men joining in the choruses, until suddenly I was very, very tired. The men had been so appreciative and generous with their applause that I kept on long after I should have rested. But what was I to do when a Scottish voice called from the audience, "Bless ye, ye're a bonny wee lass, and d'ye ken 'Ye Banks and Braes?'"

It was that old missionary spirit again: I was all aglow with the feeling of having done something for someone, but I spoke up and asked, "Isn't there someone here who can relieve me for a while? Play, or sing, or tell a story?"

A middle-aged, shy looking man named Lewis stood up and said, "That's the smallest organ I ever saw, but I'll try if you like."

I gladly but doubtfully relinquished my chair. As he seated himself, he turned to the audience and called, "Come away you, Williams, Davies and you, Rhys, and give me a bit of help, the little lady needs a rest."

I should have known that where there was a Lewis to play the organ there would be a Welsh quartet. Lewis, I discovered afterwards, held a high musical degree from the Royal Conservatory of Music in London, England, had been organist in a church in Wales, and afterwards in Winnipeg, before joining the staff of the railway company as a bookkeeper.

And now the Welsh quartet was singing with splendid vigour and harmony, after a few false starts. Before the evening, ended we heard two fine Scottish voices singing the songs of their native land; an Italian who sang operatic arias as easily as we sang "Home on the Range," and though his voice was rusty from disuse, it was true and strong and he sang the loved "Vesti la Giubba" in true Italian style.

Last but not least, a couple of big, bearded Russians sang songs of the old Cossacks with strong and resonant voices. To all the singers with the exception of the Russians, who were quite accustomed to singing unaccompanied, Mr. Lewis provided a spirited accompaniment, which must have surprised the bellows of that little organ.

By this time, I was a very meek girl. My vanity was whimpering and my social service spirit was in full flight. I had thought I was bringing those poor benighted men something they hadn't heard in many a day. But now a suspicion was creeping into my mind, that it wasn't music that was scarce and precious. It was women. Maybe it was because I was a young woman that made their applause almost an ovation at times, and that chivalry, or something else, made them so kind.

It was midnight before I was able to creep into my warm bed at Mrs. Marsden's tent. I fell asleep at once, waking to find her beside me with a breakfast tray with steaming coffee, ham and eggs, toast and marmalade.

By morning, the weather had turned very cold and we started home immediately after lunch. This meal itself was a treat, as our hostess had roasted two ptarmigan which she had shot a few days before. They were quite delicious. She gave us three frozen birds to take home, and we were grateful for her skill with a .22 rifle.

Another agreeable surprise awaited us when we arrived home. Harry Davies had come to the tent and had fires blazing in both stoves. He didn't understand our surprise at his thoughtfulness. "Why Doc," he said reproachfully, "you didn't think I'd let your wife come home to a cold house, did you? Got to take care of her, you know." Harry had heard of my pregnancy through the active grapevine and had appointed himself a committee of one to look after me. But,

The winter mail train which ran from October to May.

somehow, I didn't resent his care at all, knowing he was not giving it because Dan was the local preacher, but because he was being neighbourly.

The mail, carried by dog sled from the coast, had arrived while we were away, and there were letters from home on the table. Harry had gone down to the post office to bring them to us. Our Christmas parcels would arrive some time in June, after the river opened for navigation. Our first Christmas away from home had been most enjoyable, and we hadn't had time to be lonely.

"Dan," I muttered sleepily, that night after we had gone to bed, "aren't people nice!"

"Of course, silly, people are grand here as well as anywhere else. You just have to know them, that's all. Now go to sleep and tomorrow night we'll go skating on the new rink, that is, if you feel up to it.

"I'll go anyway. Having a baby doesn't mean I'm a cripple, thank goodness. Goodnight, dear." A snore was my only answer.

CHAPTER TWELVE

Ice Carnivals
and
Oranges

THE NEXT MORNING, THE SKIES WERE CLEAR and the air frosty, so the sunshine was welcome even for the few short hours of December days.

I remembered when we had been skating earlier in the season on Charleson's Lake several miles from town. Although it was only Halloween night, the ice on the lake then was from four to six inches thick, and there had been no snow to mar the surface. It is impossible to describe the brilliancy of the northern moonlight, due to the clear, dry, unpolluted air. That night, the moon shone so brightly that we could see the snow-crowned peaks of Rocher de Boule Mountain reflected in the ice, almost as clearly as they could be seen in the sky, and we could see the weeds on the lake bottom as well. It was so beautiful I wished all my friends in Ontario could share the experience with us, since I knew we could never make them believe it if we told them. It would sound like a tourist bureau advertisement.

The lake was a mile long and about a half-mile wide, and as we skimmed over the surface it was alarmingly like skating on water, until we assured ourselves it was really ice.

Just before midnight we had gathered around the bonfire on the shore and thoroughly enjoyed coffee which had been boiled over the fire, and the sandwiches we had brought with us. When the last crumb was eaten and the

January, 1912. Dan and Eva with newspaper editor C.H. Sawle and Mrs. Sawle in front of their tent home in Old Hazelton.

coffee pot empty, we piled into the sleigh which brought us to the lake, and went home happy, exhausted, and ready to sleep. There weren't enough dogs in the whole North to keep us awake that night, although the moon was sure to make them try.

Tonight, however, we were to skate in the new open-air rink which had been built on the bank of the Skeena in the town. The large sheet of ice was enclosed on all sides by a high board fence. Outside the fence were the piles of snow shovelled from the rink, making a spectators' gallery for those who only came to watch.

Around the top of the high snow wall were a few lanterns and carbide lamps, shedding a fairly good light on the ice, although their number had to be doubled for hockey games. Beyond these lights rose the whitewashed walls of the Hudson's Bay Company post, while in the background were low hills nestling at the foot of the mountain peaks, their snowy crests outlined against the midnight blue of the sky, star-studded and moonlit. It was a most breathtaking sight, and one never to be forgotten.

Charleson's Lake, not far from Hazelton Hospital. This picture was taken the morning after we had been skating on it. What appears to be a clear expanse of water is ice from four to six inches thick.

On the ice, the flash and clink of skates blended with music provided by a Native band, in which every man was a musician. To our amazement we found ourselves skating to the rhythm of Sousa marches and Strauss waltzes played with a fervour which would have surprised the composers. I was informed that the band leader had been trained by a priest, Father Morice, an early missionary, who was a most accomplished musician. He had taught many of the Natives to play instruments, to read music, and to sing. This band was a real tribute to his teaching.

Before the evening was over, it was unanimously decided to hold a fancy dress carnival during the Christmas season or as soon as possible afterwards. The next day, everyone in town who could stand up on skates was searching trunks, closets, and stores for anything that could be used as a costume. Being locked in our northern world by snow and ice, with only dog sled transportation from the outside, we had to use the material at hand. The results were really astounding.

The crowd assembled on the ice the night of the carnival presented a

Eva at a costume ball in Hazelton. Winter 1911–12.

bewildering array of originality and ingenuity. Monks gambolled with nursing sisters, Eskimos with ladies of the harem; there were cowboys, trappers, voyageurs. There was even a South Seas islander. When the latter figure appeared on the ice clad, apparently, in G-string and beads, everyone shivered. It was a relief to discover he was wearing three suits of woollen underwear — the top one dyed black — and he was as warm as anyone else.

Dan and I were dressed as a cowboy and Dutch girl, and while our costumes were undistinguished, we did win a prize for skating. We were both former hockey players. I'll remember that night as long as I live; it was such a happy one. It was a friendly crowd, warm-hearted and vigorous, and we loved them all.

Suddenly, as we skated, we were confronted with the Devil — tail, horns and all, in a black costume covered by a large red cape. The words of our old minister and his warning ". . . where Satan lifteth up his head," came back to me. "Look, Dan, here he is," I said, "the lad we've been looking for, Satan himself!" We were laughing unrestrainedly. When the time for unmasking

Hockey players. Arrow points to Jock McQueen who was shot in the November robbery. On the left, "x" is Cy North, later Major, in charge of Canadian Engineers in the 2nd World War.

came, Satan turned out to be a mild, cultured Englishman who worked in the government office.

With such a splendid rink and many months of ice, there was bound to be a hockey team. A three-cornered league came into being, including Hazelton, the new town of construction camps, and Smithers, a town about fifty miles east.

This league played very good hockey. The team members were mostly former players from professional and top amateur teams from Halifax, Ottawa, Montreal, Winnipeg, and Rossland, who had drifted into the North to jobs in banks, offices, and railway construction. They played for the glory of their team and were loyally backed by local supporters. During the hockey season, we were all violently partisan, friendships were forgotten, and loyalty was the only virtue we knew. We loved our own team and had nothing but contempt for the others. Everyone who could walk attended the games.

On several occasions, spectators fell onto the ice from the top of the snowy grandstand. One night, a wheelbarrow was hurled down directly into the path of the fastest skater on the Smithers team. Another night, a player with the construction workers had the top of his ear sliced off when he was boarded by an opponent; and once a skull was fractured right in front of me. If I had not seen the uplifted stick in time, I might have been the victim, as I was leaning forward in the front row in my excitement.

Although the hockey games were attended by everyone, the twenty or more women living in town by this time each had a "day" when she would serve afternoon tea for the others, who made the rounds, visiting everyone at least once a month. Each hostess tried to outdo the others in making good things to eat from the scanty stores available, and these events were quite a social success. We sat exchanging recipes, gorging ourselves, and indulging in harmless (sometimes) gossip.

As the winter wore away my appetite went with it, and by spring it was non-existent. One more piece of ham or bacon, one more stale egg, another can of corn or tomatoes, and I expected insanity to overtake me.

Hugh and Tom McKay had returned from their winter of trapping, and would soon be returning to the mountains for a summer of prospecting. They were our guests at supper one evening and on leaving, Hughie, bashful and rather red of face, said, "Hope you're feelin' well, Mrs. Doc. Noticed you didn't eat much. Have to take care of the little fella you know!"

I was astonished but managed to thank him. "You are very kind to notice, Hugh, but somehow food seems very dry. I'm just waiting for the boats to start running so I can get some fresh fruit or green vegetables."

"Don't bring much fruit on the first couple of boats, Ma'am, mostly booze for Black Jack at the hotel. It's a darn shame!"

"Well, I expect I'll survive, but I would give anything for a fresh egg or an orange," I said.

"Don't blame you a mite," said Tom, who was more bashful than Hugh, but always beamed friendliness.

When the two men had gone I asked Dan, "How in the world did Hugh know we were going to have a baby? Did you tell him?"

Old Hazelton in winter.

"Take a look at yourself, my girl!" he answered. "How could he help knowing?"

Three mornings later I heard the joyful whistle of the boat as it chugged slowly up the river. I was lying on the couch, trying to keep my coffee and toast down, feeling like a sunken barge, and life seemed grim. I must have fallen asleep when a loud knock at the tent door made me sit up quickly. "Come in," I cried.

The door opened and Hugh and Tom came in, carrying a large box which they brought over and set down at my feet. It was a crate of oranges. While I tried to sob out my thanks, the men fled from the tent without a word.

Never in my life had I seen anything so beautiful! The lid was loose and in ten seconds I was gulping down a juicy orange, scarcely waiting to peel it properly. Just then Dan came in.

"What on earth have you got there? Where did it come from?"

"Oranges," I mumbled with my mouth full. "Hughie and Tom brought them, and I was crying so hard I scared them out before I had time to thank them. Have one, this is my third."

"I went down to the trading post to try to get some fruit for you," Dan said, "but they said there was none on board, so how did the boys get these?" I didn't know, and they had not told me.

The mystery was partly explained when Hugh later admitted getting the oranges from the boat's cook. We never knew whether the boys just took them when the cook wasn't looking or whether they bought them. If they did buy them, they probably paid enough to send the cook on a world tour. But all my finer feelings were sternly repressed for the time being, and I didn't care how the oranges had been procured. I just ate them and was thankful.

CHAPTER 13

A Frontier Rescue

As the days of spring wore away and summer neared, I felt decidedly uncomfortable. What strange fancies take possession of mothers in the last months before the birth of their children: I wanted an egg. A fresh egg. There wasn't a fresh egg to be found in the stores. Then someone told me that a certain Chinese, who had a small store in the heart of the oldest part of the town, owned a couple of hens. I decided to interview the Chinese merchant — with a fresh egg as my objective.

Down a little back alley I wandered, alert for the sight of a hen. To my delight, I saw one meandering along, aimlessly at first, then walking faster as she watched me approach. I chased her for a few yards until she disappeared into a small shed. I entered the back door of the store opposite the shed and found two Chinese playing cards. Nervously I asked the one facing me, "Have you any fresh eggs?"

"No, Missy, no eggs!" And the game went on.

"I saw a hen out there and she went into your shed. Are you sure she hasn't laid an egg?"

"Oh, maybe she lay one pretty soon. You want egg?"

"I certainly do! Please, please let me have it if there is one. Will you go and see?" He went out and came back in a minute with three eggs. I asked, "Does your hen lay three eggs at one time?"

He laughed. "Maybe I have fi' six hen. You pay me?"

"Indeed I will. How much?"

"One dolla, three eggs. O.K.?"

"Here's your dollar. Thanks ever so much." I almost snatched the eggs from him and started for home. They tasted like ambrosia to me, almost as good as the oranges.

By this time the freight camp where the horses and mules were stabled between trips, had been moved eastward beyond Hazelton and Dan was spending much of his time at the new location. The company had built a new hospital for him, and he had to be there to see that all the necessary equipment had been provided. He had permission to order everything he might need in the way of drugs, medicines, and instruments. In fact, so important was the animals' welfare, that he found himself provided with much better housing and equipment than were the employees' medical doctors. But then, labour was plentiful and cheap, and horses were expensive.

Being alone so much, my temper became distinctly ragged. How else can a woman feel when she is swathed in a tent-like garment especially designed for maternity in the style of the early 1900s. Mother had ordered it for me from Eatons in Toronto, and it was too large for me even in my eighth month of pregnancy. The gowns of those days resembled nothing so much as a half-opened umbrella, and when I saw myself in the mirror I wanted to weep for my long-lost figure.

When Dan did come home for a few days I called him "Doctor," knowing well it would annoy him. It did, and he spoke sharply, "Good heavens, Eve, why call me that? You're not one of the men on the job you know. You're my wife!"

But I was piqued, and would have my say. "Well, it seemed a little familiar to call you by your first name when I see so little of you," I said with some sarcasm. "Perhaps, when we are better acquainted . . ."

The hospital where Margaret and Marian were born, located between Old and New towns.

Dan looked at me for a minute, then said gently, "You're having a rough time, I know." When I nodded my head with tears in my eyes, he said, "I wish I didn't have to leave you so much, but this settles it! You are going to the hospital to stay until the baby comes. The doctor told me I should take you there as soon as possible, since I have to be away."

The Hazelton hospital was situated about two miles east of the town, along the Aldermere road. It was established several years before we arrived by the Methodist Church of Canada to serve the needs of the people, both Native and white, in the Upper Skeena Valley.

The superintendent, Dr. H.C. Wrinch, was a medical missionary, and he had administered to the needs of the people, day and night, travelling far afield many times to bring treatment to those who were unable to come to the hospital.

Into that place of healing poured a steady stream of sick, injured, and those enfeebled by age. Babies were born there, while others, whose days were numbered, passed by on their way to eternity. Life and death, youth and old age, pain and soothing, were all within the four walls.

A nursing superintendent and five nurses, a housekeeper, and several assistants in wards, kitchen, and garden, took care of the patients. There was also a house surgeon always in attendance.

Young mothers were taught how to care for their babies, the correct methods of bathing, dressing, and feeding them. The mothers were regaled with chicken broth and fresh eggs from the chicken pens of the doctor's wife. It was worth having a baby in that hospital to be so well fed.

One ward was devoted to alcoholic patients trying to get rid of pink elephants and other horrible visions. I recall one who was relentlessly pursued and smothered by salmon all the time his delirium lasted. He used to shout, "get your fishy tails out of my mouth!" to the great amusement of the nurses. These cases were given not only the necessary medical treatment, but were soundly scolded by the nurses when the time came for them to leave, looking ashamed and crestfallen. Since the nurses were almost the only single women in the place, their good opinion was most eagerly sought. Many were the promises of good behaviour, apologies, and requests for further attention, given them.

There were tennis courts on the lawn and all Hazelton's eligible males — and there were a good many — developed a passion for tennis. Although the nurses received training of a high order, not all the graduates made use of their diplomas. Only very agile young women could hope to escape the matrimonial nets spread for their unwary feet, luring them to housekeeping jobs when their training was completed.

The greatest problem, however, was to take care of those who were either too far away or too ill to come to the hospital. Today, a radio message is sent out, the patient is carried to the nearest lake or field, a helicopter soars overhead, lands, and with the patient aboard, flies to a hospital in a few hours. Eighty or so years ago, such journeys meant days of dangerous and painful travelling to attend the suffering or to bring them to the hospital.

In the fall of 1912, word was brought that a man was seriously ill at Fourth Cabin, nearly one hundred miles north of Hazelton, on the old Telegraph Trail to the Yukon. At once the house doctor, a young man named Charles G.

MacLean, a recent graduate from medical college, volunteered to go and minister to the sick man, or bring him to the hospital if necessary.

He knew nothing whatever about travelling on foot over mountain trails, but since it was necessary for someone to go, he hesitated not a moment, but immediately prepared for the journey. He took another man with him, but this man had never been over these mountains and was unfamiliar with the trail.

They set out on horseback and arrived at First Cabin that evening, after almost thirty miles of riding. They planned to spend the night there, as they were both very tired. As they prepared for bed that night, a party of prospectors arrived, and spread their blankets on the floor too. The doctor and his guide were amused to see the men hang their shoes from the rafters on strings. The doctor and his friend placed theirs on the floor beside them. In the morning they were not amused at all. During the night, rats had eaten every one of the rawhide laces. Fortunately, the telegraph operator had some spare shoelaces which he gave them. After this experience, they also hung their shoes from the rafters.

From the First Cabin on, the trails were impassable for horses, so they turned their mounts into a mountain pasture and continued their journey on foot. Wearily they climbed, carrying their packs containing food, blankets, dry socks, and a medical bag fitted out with supplies for almost any emergency. Teeth clenched, feet blistered, they kept going, hour after hour, until there appeared, almost magically it seemed, a little cabin with smoke curling up from the chimney. The doctor told me later, "It looked to us like the Pearly Gates, with Heaven just behind! We were so tired we could hardly speak to the old prospector who opened the door to us. He took one look, and motioned us to come in. We slumped into the homemade armchairs, almost asleep on our feet, and without a word he made a big pot of very strong tea. We drank every drop of it." He shook his head and smiled, "I didn't know anything in the world could revive a man so quickly as that tea did, or taste so good." I told him a testimonial like that would be worth a good deal to some tea company, but he said, "It was such a lifesaver to us, they can have it for nothing!"

After resting for the night, they continued on their way until they finally reached Third Cabin. One more long day and they arrived at their destination. The sick man was examined almost immediately by the doctor, who found him suffering from an advanced mastoid; there was nothing to be done until the patient could be taken to the hospital. There he would have an operation which was impossible to perform elsewhere. How to get him to the hospital was the problem.

Almost providentially, it seemed, the answer arrived within a few hours. A Campbell-Johnson survey party came along on their way to Hazelton, and the men volunteered to help carry the patient to the hospital.

A stretcher was made at once, consisting of poles, canvas, and blankets, and with the man under the influence of an opiate, the party started on their long and difficult journey.

The trail, which was dangerous enough walking in single file, became a nightmare for men carrying a stretcher. The sharp curves, high on the mountainside, had to be rounded very carefully lest the stretcher poles brush the men over the side. Hour after hour they walked, changing bearers often so as to make the best possible time.

They crossed Poison Mountain, so called because of the hundreds of horses and mules that had died there from eating poisonous weeds growing on the slopes on the overland trail to the Yukon in '98. Next came a mountain which brought deep curses from every man who crossed it. There were several little bridges spanning crevices in the rocks, which were so rickety the men almost held their breath until once more they felt solid rock beneath their feet. Looking downward over the edge of the trail, they occasionally noted the whitened bones of some packhorse, or possibly those of the packer himself. It was a frightening journey but they moved step by step downward toward the lower plateau and the wider trail where they were to make camp for the night. "That was the mountain called the S.O.B.," the doctor told me. "It was named by the first men who travelled it and it is still called by that name," he said. "Believe me, Mrs. MacLean, those letters describe it exactly. It's really one S.O.B.!"

As the men built a fire that evening and prepared their supper, the doctor kept a close watch on his patient, hoping to keep him alive until they reached the hospital, and a possible chance for life. He then removed his boots to treat his bruised and blistered feet. It was the first time he had worn heavy mountaineering boots, and his tender feet were a mass of blisters. He took time to soak them in the cool water, then applied ointment and a few bandages. But he put his shoes back on immediately. "If I had left them off for an hour I don't think I would have been able to put them on again," he said.

He had suffered intense pain, but still had kept up with those seasoned men of the mountain country, much to their surprise and admiration.

When the cavalcade reached First Cabin again, the two men mounted their horses with a long sigh of relief and rode the rest of the way. In a little over five days from Fourth Cabin, they carried the patient into the Hazelton hospital, and gave him over into the hands of Dr. Wrinch and the nurses.

The man who had at first been called the "Tenderfoot Doc," went to bed for forty-eight hours to give his feet a chance to heal. From then on he was called, almost affectionately, Doctor Charlie. Dr. MacLean was later a Canadian Army medical officer on duty at the Vancouver Veterans' Hospital.

Although he shared the family surname, Doctor Charlie was not related to my husband, but their mutual ancestors came originally from the Isle of Mull.

Very few of the hospital staff from that era are still living, and the old building has been torn down to make way for a new and more modern hospital. However, the children who were born in that first hospital in the Skeena Valley, are proud to remember their birthplace in that house of healing.

CHAPTER FOURTEEN

The Mayor
of
Manson Creek

AND SO IT HAPPENED THAT A FEW DAYS LATER I found myself installed in a private room in the hospital, where the nurses were quite accustomed to the sight of shapeless dresses and woebegone faces.

The days passed more pleasantly for me, but the waiting period seemed long until my baby girl was born, three weeks overdue. It seemed to me that the doctor's methods were outdated, and he was more missionary than medical. When my time came and the baby still refused to be born, in extreme agony I begged for an anesthetic, but he told me sternly, "You will just have to bear it Mrs. MacLean. We are all born in travail, and birth is woman's most wonderful experience."

I had enough travail in the next ten hours to make him change his mind, and the last four hours I was on the operating table. Somehow I was unable to find birth a wonderful experience, thanks to him and his religious scruples about the purifying effect of pain. He really was a Torquemada!

Dan stayed in town for a week and visited me every day. Because he was my only visitor, I watched the window anxiously to see him riding up the avenue to the hospital. He rode Frank, a very high-spirited saddle horse which the company had assigned to him, because he was the only staff member with the experience to handle such a horse. Frank was a magnificent animal although he staged a one-horse rodeo every time he was saddled. It always took a couple of miles to calm him down, and I was thankful when Dan dismounted and was on his way to my room.

We named our baby Margaret, and when she was three weeks old we went home to the tent. I was still far from well and doing my house work as well as looking after the baby was too much for me. The only help obtainable was from a Chinese boy Dan found somewhere; this person couldn't speak English, neither had he ever done housework in his life. My neighbours helped me a great deal, bringing me dainty food and taking my laundry home with them. They then brought it back washed and nicely ironed. True, I was flooded with advice about taking care of Margaret, but I had learned not to resent advice.

A retired miner, Charlie MacKinnon, lived in a cabin not far from our tent at the time. He was a Scot, well over eighty, and a crusty old man. In his younger days, he had taken a Native wife and together they raised a large family. When white men began to arrive in great numbers, Charlie felt embarrassed to be found with a Native wife and family, so he sent them all back to her tribe. After knowing Charlie for a year or two, I was convinced that the choice of home had been hers, because he could be very disagreeable at times. He was a big man with a full white beard, white hair and a ruddy complexion which made him look like Santa Claus. His prospecting days were over, so he seemed at a loss to know what to do with his time, and always stopped in for a while as he passed the tent on his way home from a walk. He seemed very fond of the baby and gave enthusiastic advice, which I seldom followed. One evening, I persuaded him to stay for supper, and he seemed very much pleased. As I was preparing a bottle of milk for Margaret, he could stand it no longer and shouted at me, "Milk! Milk! Nothin' but milk! She'll never grow on that stuff! Feed her taties and onions and good red meat. I tell ye there's no good in milk."

Charlie had been in the hospital at the time my baby was born, recovering from an attack of bronchitis under the care of the doctor and nurses, who found him a very impatient patient. As he recovered, his mind was still wandering and his nurses treated him as they would a child. The doctor allowed him only one pipeful of tobacco a day, which was agony for the poor old fellow, and he failed to see what kindness it was to take a man's pipe away from him. He slept poorly and at night, when the hospital was quiet and the nurse downstairs, he would get up and wander around in search of his pipe and tobacco.

My sleeping was frequently disturbed, too, and I was awake one night when I heard the soft slap of bare feet walking slowly down the hall towards my door. Before I could ring for the nurse, Charlie stood in my door way in his short nightshirt. As he entered, walking feebly, he was muttering, "Dang them nurses! Can't find my pipe! Them danged interfering women! Take my pipe, take away my tobacco! Wait till I get out of here, I'll fix em, so I will!" As I rang the bell the old man bent over the bed, "Don't be skeered, little lady, old Charlie won't hurt you. Got any tobacco? I just want a smoke and them dang nurses won't let me!"

"You'd better get back to bed, Mr. MacKinnon, or the nurse will catch you running about like this," I warned him.

"Hey there, Charlie!" came the nurse's voice from the doorway. "What do you mean coming in here and scaring Mrs. MacLean like this?"

"Didn't mean to scare her none, just asked fer some tobacco," he replied.

"All right then, come along back to bed and get some sleep," and she led him away.

Charlie was only one of the old-timers who interested us. They were fine old men who had spent most of their adult life in one gold camp after another. They came from Sacramento, from Barkerville, and then to Manson Creek in 1869. Ten years seemed to be about the life of a gold boom at its height. There were several of these retired miners now living in Hazelton, such as Jim May, Ezra Evans, Charlie MacKinnon, as well as men who had been traders and packers and others of associated work.

Of them all, Jim May was easily the leader, as he had been in Manson Creek where he was known as "The Mayor." He was a soft-spoken man, kept his head under most circumstances, and was wise in the ways of outdoorsmen.

Retirement age in the North came when miners were no longer able to work their claims or pursue gold further. If they had found enough to take care of

Dan and Eva with their first child,
Margaret, born August 8, 1912 at
Old Hazelton.

themselves in their old age, that was good, but if there was a possibility of finding more, they stayed at the game as long as possible.

One old prospector who died just before we arrived in Hazelton was known as "Cactus Jack." We never knew his surname as his nickname was all that appeared on his grave marker; however, below his name and the date of his death, were inscribed in large letters the words, "God is Love." This is the story we were told about him.

Cactus Jack was a hardworking and an honest man, but so grouchy and irritable that other men avoided him. His leisure time in Hazelton was spent for the most part in fishing, or at least sitting by a stream with a rod in his hand. He had one habit which was known to everyone: he was always chewing tobacco. Other men said the only time he wasn't chewing was when he was sleeping or eating, and they weren't sure of that!

As he advanced in age, he fell ill with a very bad cold which turned to bronchitis, and the doctor was called to his cabin. Dr. Wrinch came and tried to take his temperature. He found it difficult to persuade Jack to open his mouth. The Doctor, who never forgot he was also a missionary, immediately gave him a lecture on the sin of chewing tobacco, and told him he would have to get rid of it immediately if he wished to be cured. Jack eyed him resentfully and answered, "Doc, when I ain't got any terbaccy in my jaw, I'll be dead anyway, so what's the difference?"

So Cactus Jack died, although the doctor did everything he could for him except take his temperature. Jack would not open his mouth.

After his burial, one man who knew Jack well carved a headboard with the inscription, his name and the date of his death.

When he was asked why he put "God is Love" on the head-board, he said emphatically, "I wrote that because I think God will have to be plumb full of love to let old Cactus into heaven."

Ezra was a Welshman who came to Canada as a young man. He had been attending medical college in Wales, but he had failed his examinations at the end of the second year. Discouraged, he decided to follow many of his friends to the new world in the West. He arrived first in California, and had to find work of some kind if he was to go any further. When he heard of some men who were going to take camels to the Barkerville gold fields, where they would be used, he signed on as a helper. The tales of the camel train are many, but the men got as far north as Clinton in the interior of southern British Columbia. The trouble started when a horse packtrain arrived at almost the same time, coming south from Barkerville. When the horses met the camels, pandemonium broke loose. The camels took flight to the east, and the horses to the woods on the other side of the road. There was no stopping either group, and the camels never stopped their headlong rush until finally they reached the prairie country and the low hills around Ashcroft, where they were sighted days later. The horse train ran just as wildly through the thick forest, knocking their packs against trees, losing them all over the wooded country. It is said that the men of the camel train spent at least three days rounding up their animals and some of the packs were never found. Ezra never enjoyed hearing anyone mentioning his first entry into the north land, but he managed to find

Well-known prospectors Jim May (left) and Ezra Evans in front of Evans' cabin. Anglican church just behind it.

his way to Barkerville. He spent many years there and in the Omineca until he retired and came to live in Hazelton.

Ezra was highly esteemed by his fellows, and later, when he fell ill, his two closest friends, Jim May and Charlie MacKinnon, used to walk to his cabin every evening to sit with him. Jim said, "He's just a lad and he needs us." At this time Jim was 83, Charlie MacKinnon 81, and Ezra was only 78.

During his years in the Manson Creek gold camp in the Omineca country, he became the mining recorder, and his medical knowledge was of great service in a land of few doctors.

Most of the miners were friends from years of association in Barkerville, or possibly Sacramento, and they made their deals and transfers, sealing the bargains with firm handshakes. Sometimes, Ezra would make records of transactions without their knowledge, and with one pretext or another he would persuade them to write their names on a piece of paper although they scorned written agreements. Unfortunately, there were many dishonest men, and Ezra was unable to save some miners from having claims jumped by speculators.

The spring of 1912 found Ezra with his packhorse loaded with his outfit and the saddle on his pony, off to Manson Creek for one more year in the place he loved. He started out, against the advice of his friends, but became ill, fell off his horse, and found himself unable to mount again, although the pony and packhorse stood quietly beside him. He was found lying by the side of the road not far from Hazelton and brought home to his bed. Ezra died a few weeks later and was buried in the presence of the whole town. Everyone grieved at the passing of such a man, and there was no such inscription on his headboard as was carved on Jack's, because no one could imagine God not wanting Ezra in Heaven.

As for Jim May, he had lived such an adventurous life that it would take many pages to tell his story. Dan had many a long talk with him, listening to the story of his travels. He said he had walked all the way to Manson Creek from his home in Tennessee. His family left their home there to take the long trek across the continent to the gold fields of Sacramento. Jim told him, "We had a couple of cows and a spare mule walkin' behind the wagon. And I was the one who had to herd them along, so I walked most of the way out there. When we heard of the gold strike in Barkerville, I walked to San Francisco and got a boat to Victoria, and from there to Yale. Then I walked from there to Barkerville, and ten years later I walked to Manson Creek, so I guess you could say I walked most of the way."

There is a story about his stay in Barkerville which really must be told. A banquet was being held in honour of several mining men and officials from the provincial government, and the best known and most popular of the miners were invited to attend. Among them was Jim, who had two sets of clothes which he alternated wearing. These consisted of blue denims or woollen pants, dark shirts, knee-length rubber boots, and two jackets, one for summer and one for winter. The other men told him he would have to dress up for the banquet, but they met with fierce opposition. Jim simply refused to wear a store suit, collar and tie, or even leather boots, as the other men did.

His friends would not give up, and went to the trading posts until they found a suit which would fit a man who was six feet four inches tall and of sturdy build. They brought the suit to Jim's cabin, and ten men came with it to see that Jim put it on. The fight which ensued, they say, was one that would never be forgotten in Barkerville.

Jim arrived at the banquet arrayed in the store suit and the other accessories, and the ten men were with him, all wearing decorations in the shape of black eyes, swollen noses, cracked ribs, and bruised fists. It was the first and only time Jim wore the suit. Nobody knew what became of it, but when we knew Jim many years later, he was still wearing the blue denims, dark shirts, and high rubber boots.

One old-timer in town was not so popular as the men. He was a sassy little donkey. He had been left in town by one of the prospectors who came through on the overland trail to the Yukon in '98. The man had been delayed in town because one of his burro train gave birth to a son. Since he could not take the little burro with him, one family had volunteered to keep the animal as a pet for their children. By this time, Johnny was the pet and the pest of Hazelton. He had the idea that he could go anywhere and do anything he chose, and he preferred gardens, as he could eat anything in them. One day, I returned from the village to find him calmly eating all the bright flowers in the nasturtium boxes outside my neighbours' tent. I attacked him with a big stick, but he paid no attention except to switch his tail at every blow. Then Dan came along and saw what was happening. He took a bottle of the hottest liniment there is, out of his surgical bag, and applied some of it to the tenderest part of Johnny's anatomy. With a wild bray, Johnny leaped into the air and ran, hee-hawing wildly, through the gate and down the hill. The liniment only stung for a moment, and would do him no harm, but he never came back to our enclosure.

Dan had news for me a few days later. "Eve, we're going to have to move

Construction camp at Skeena Crossing, building the new railway bridge.

to the new construction town, New Hazelton, near the Bulkley Canyon. They are building me a hospital camp there, and we will have to be nearer to it." And so we moved our tent and started again to make a home.

CHAPTER FIFTEEN

A Pierrot Show
and the
Tug-o'-war
Caper

NEW HAZELTON WAS SITUATED about five miles from the old town, one mile and a half west of the Bulkley Canyon at Hagwilget village. There were two bridges spanning the Bulkley, a low level bridge on the main road, and the famous Old Indian Bridge, at Hagwilget, which had been built many years before by the Natives under the guidance of Father Morice, then priest in charge of the Catholic missions on the Upper Skeena. The bridge was built with wooden pegs in place of nails, and held together with ropes of cedar bark twisted into unbelievable strength. Suspended above, and attached by these ropes, was a large cable which had been used by the Hudson's Bay Company for lining its boats up river in the time of high water.

One old story, concocted by white men to belittle the Natives, had it that when the bridge was finished, the Natives sent six of their heaviest women to the centre to test its strength. That story is untrue; the bridge's strength was tested by a pony packtrain, crossing slowly, one by one, under the supervision of the government agent.

Some of the Old Hazelton shops and businesses had moved to the new town, but most of the residents were connected with the building of the railway and they were strangers to me. Dan knew most of them because of his work, so it was but a short time, before I, too, became acquainted.

Old Hagwilget Bridge, built by hand by the Natives.

Hagwilget Bridge, a different view.

It was October when we moved, and the long twilight was upon us. Our tent was set up on what was rather grandly called Tenth Avenue. The main road through the village was called Pugsley Street, and it stretched from the construction headquarters to the foot of Rocher de Boule mountain. This beautiful mountain dominated the whole valley for many miles around, with its rich colouring of copper tones, green trees, and snow-capped peaks. Most of the businesses were on Pugsley Street, including the poolroom, two general stores, a cafe, a laundry and a rooming house. Log cabins, tents, and larger houses were on the short side streets running north and south from Pugsley Street. These streets were roughly constructed through stumps, trees, and boulders which were difficult to remove, so the plank walks were laid around some of them. These obstacles were hard to locate in the dark, and one often found oneself astride low stumps until their locations became familiar.

The rooming house, which was owned by Arizona Smith, was the main social centre for the construction workers. The large downstairs room was filled with tables and chairs to accommodate the nightly poker sessions. It was an oasis in the desert of great distances and hard work, bringing rest and relaxation to men far from home, although some times the relaxation was overdone. There were quarrels over the games, as in any gambling establishment, and the noise occasionally alarmed passersby.

Sometimes, as I walked by the establishments, I could see as many as a hundred men sitting at the tables, or walking around watching the players, bottles on the table, the air blue with smoke. I was glad the good people back home couldn't see it as they would have been more certain than ever that New Hazelton was really Satan's abode. Such games in eastern Ontario took place behind closed doors; here, the doors were always open, the windows unshaded, and the whole town was welcome to come in and share the fun.

I walked without fear, because I knew that nobody would harm me. The wives — there were no single women in the town then — were respected and protected, even placed on some sort of pedestal by some who, in different surroundings might have proved troublesome. The code of the North protected the weak.

There was a district on the edge of town where the men turned for other entertainment, but in occasional conversation with one of the prostitutes, I found that most of them had decided to remain in the North and that they would never go back to cities, where they received much less tolerance and kindness. Some of the prostitutes eventually married, settled down, and raised families of good citizens.

The new town flourished and became a hive of activity. Money was plentiful and flowed in a steady stream into and out of the people's pockets. Dan's first job was to find a place to hold church services. A tent was erected and was soon fitted up with the chairs that Bill Morrison had left with us when he closed the YMCA mission in that district.

Dan was leaving for Old Hazelton immediately after the first service in the tent, so the sled dogs were harnessed and placed in a small shed nearby. Because this was the first service of any kind held in the new town, the tent was filled to capacity. As we rose to sing the opening hymn, "I to the Hills Will Lift Mine Eyes," the trouble began. Teddy, the dog who was seven-eighths wolf, had never heard massed singing before, and his ear for music was either very good, or very bad. He began to howl loudly and mournfully. The community spirit being what it is in dogs, Bob, Nick, and Bildad (whom we had recovered from his previous owner), joined in chorus with Teddy. Before the second verse was well begun, all the other dogs in town had joined the concert in a very noisy serenade. The din was ear-splitting and the only way we knew we were singing was because our lips were moving. As we "lifted our eyes to the hills" the howls of the dogs rose much higher. A young girl ran to the shed to try to quiet the animals, but the moment she opened the door they bolted, knocking her down, and ran for the woods, harness and all, and did not return for hours. Dan was forced to saddle his horse and ride to his next service.

There is this much to be said for dogs. The average congregational singing of hymns is usually doleful enough to make a person howl, quietly at least, but there was nothing restrained about Teddy and his mates, and when their sensibilities were wounded, they were willing to let the whole world know. From then on, the dogs were kept at a safe distance from the church tent.

Presbyterian church where Dan preached in New Hazelton.

New Hazelton became a lively spot with some sort of entertainment or sport almost every week. For a town of less than two hundred souls, there was an astonishing amount of talent. A group of singers and actors began to hold rehearsals in readiness for future entertainment. A tennis court was levelled off as soon as the snow had disappeared in the spring, and when the long days of sunlight began, we played tennis almost every evening.

On May 24, New Hazelton held its first celebration. A full program was planned, and all those living in the surrounding country invited to be our guests. There were horse races in the morning, a baseball game in the afternoon, and in the evening a variety concert and dance. The hotel, a new one built by Black Jack MacDonell, offered a banquet for the visitors, and the town was in holiday mood. When the day's sports were over, the banquet eaten, the curtains were raised promptly at eight o'clock in the hall where the concert and dance were to be held. This hall was the ground floor of Arizona Smith's rooming house, which had been cleared for the occasion and a stage built. Benches were thrown together, chairs borrowed, and boxes and even upturned pails were used for seats.

The concert was a Pierrot show, with six young men and six young women (all married), dressed in Pierrot costumes, black and white for the men, and scarlet and black for the women. The stage wings were hung with black and white curtains and the drop curtain was scarlet. It was a colourful setting, but we were appalled when the bills came in for our costumes, sheer stockings and rosetted slippers. When the curtain rose, however, we sent up a prayer of thankfulness. The hall was crowded to the door, and with the price of admission at seventy-five cents, our expenses were covered and we settled down to give our best performance.

Between the acts of the musical Pierrot show, we staged a mock breach of promise trial, based on the new theme song, "You Made Me Love You," a sketch written by Ray Fenton, a bank clerk. Hearing this song more recently, Dan and I found it unrecognizable in its modern dress, tortured and distorted out of all resemblance from the original. But that night it was sung by the wife of one of our best hockey players, a Victoria woman who had sung many leading roles in musical comedy, and hers was a splendid performance. Fenton, a recent arrival from England, had been trained with one of the best amateur theatrical groups in his home city. He was our stage manager and was a fairly good tenor singer as well. His greatest accomplishment, however, was his skill in make-up. He rouged, powdered, pencilled, and creamed us until we scarcely knew ourselves or each other. But this professional touch had quite an effect on the audience.

A railroad contractor from the eastern section asked one man after the show, "Where did this troupe come from? It must have cost a pretty penny to bring them from the coast!"

It was an unfortunate question to ask that particular man. He was a good Presbyterian, and his wife had been one of the troupe. He thought make-up was sinful under any circumstances. He didn't answer the question, but turned away, and was heard to mutter, "Disgraceful!"

When the bills were paid, seventy-five cents remained as profit, so we bought a box of chocolates to eat at our wind-up meeting. The show must have been enjoyable, as we had many requests for more entertainment.

In spite of all this social life — concerts, teas, and tennis — I was very lonely. At first, Dan had made only occasional trips to the camps, but now he was making only occasional trips home. His workload was heavy as there were hundreds of horses and mules on the construction sites, and the work was dangerous everywhere through the mountains. There were endless accidents and he slaved night and day.

Dan attempted to provide a certain amount of social service and guidance for the men, but found it was difficult as they ignored not only Dan, but the other ministers who came through occasionally; his only friends knew him as "Doc." Church services were an impossibility, but he managed to hold one evening meeting in the bar of a stopping place along the way, when he persuaded about eighty men to listen to him.

Whether it be in army or civilian construction camps, when hundreds of men are gathered in isolation from their families there are bound to be camp followers, blind pigs, prostitutes, professional gamblers, and all kinds of other parasites. The Grand Trunk Pacific Railway camp was no exception, and they were in full force. Dan felt that a talk on the effects of some pastimes might be timely, and painted a somewhat gruesome picture for the restless men.

A few left the meeting, but most stayed, some thanking him warmly at the end of his talk. But that wasn't the whole result. A week later, one of the freight skinners met him in the barn, and grinned widely as he told him, "Hey Doc! You sure raised hell with your lecture the other night. Since listening to all the God-awful things you said, the men have been pretty scared, so damn virtuous, in fact, that the girls have cut their prices in half. But don't forget, they're after your scalp! Didn't like it, nohow."

Dan just laughed. "Wait until you hear what I have for you the next time. I'll have you boys walking the straight and narrow yet!"

"Gosh, Doc, we gotta have a little fun," the man protested.

"Sure, I know you have, but take it easier and don't kill yourselves with fun. Dead men don't have much to enjoy."

"Is it true, Doc, we're gonna have a sports day, Saturday? I sure like tug-o'-war. Hope there's goin' to be one."

"You bet we will," Dan said. "It's my favourite sport too. We'll have it right here in camp where everyone will have a chance."

When Saturday afternoon came, there were several hundred men gathered in the clearing beside the camp. The ground was rough, with plenty of stumps, but they managed to find a fairly clear space for their tug-o'-war. There were many Europeans working on the grade, Russians, Serbs, Montenegrins — big fellows, strong and heavy. There were also many Scots, not quite so large, but trained in the art of pulling on a rope. The contest was Scots against the world!

Teams were chosen, eight "oatmeal eaters" averaging about 180 pounds each, against the men of the European team, who averaged nearer to 225 pounds apiece. The Scots had to put their brains, training, and experience against an overwhelming weight advantage. After a minute or two, it looked as though experience would count, but when it became obvious that their team was losing to the smaller men, the Europeans added helpers, one after another, to their end of the rope until there were at least a dozen pulling.

Dan was in the loop for the Scots, being one of the heaviest, and when he saw the aid being received by the other team, he had a bright idea. Just behind him there was a little green stump about two feet high and ten inches across. He edged closer to it, slipped the rope over its top, and settled down to hold.

A hectic battle ensued. When there was no more room on the rope the Europeans seized their men by their waists and pulled, but no matter what they did, they couldn't budge the Scots. Finally, there were so many on the European team they got in each other's way. The front men gave up and rolled to the ground. Dan stood up, slipping the rope off the stump as he did so, and the Scots were victorious. The land of Bruce the Persistent, Wallace the Warrior, Bobbie the Bard, and Angus McAskill, was victorious. Scotland's honour was safe. The story of that victory was told throughout the valley, but this is the first time the secret has been disclosed. Some of the men were discussing the game in the camp that night, and the little Italian boy who took care of the saddle horses heard them and was sorely troubled by the defeat of the old world warriors. He, too, had suffered, as the English-speaking men in the camp often teased him about his broken English, and called him "Dago." Dan found him weeping bitterly in the stall beside his own pony.

"What's the matter, Tony, are you sick?"

"No, Doc, not sick, justa mad! Too many Scotchmen here, all McLeods, McKays, McLeans, McTavishes, and Sandy Morrison, all come from same place Jacka Stewart. Nobody here but da Scotchmen for da Christ's sake," and his tears broke forth afresh.

When Dan came home he told me about Tony. "You know, Eve," he said, "I felt like crying myself, and it certainly made me think! We call ourselves Canadians, Americans, Scots, Irish or English, and call all the rest of the world the most contemptuous names — Hunkies, Dagoes, Frogs, Niggers, Chinks, Japs. Funny, isn't it, when according to the Bible we are all descended from Adam. I wonder why we feel so superior? We aren't really. We only think we are."

"Perhaps if we became better acquainted with the rest of the world we might change our ways," I said. "For instance Mary, who washes my clothes for me, is one of the nicest persons I know. She surprises me with her kindly wit and humour. But why should I be surprised just because she is a Native? There are plenty of women of our own race who have neither wit nor humour, and I don't give it a thought."

Our friend, Harry Davies from Hazelton, was visiting us when this conversation took place. He sat smoking quietly while we talked. Then he said, "Aye, lad, this big country up here is a grand place for us to learn that all men are human and even the worst of them have some good."

He puffed away for a little while, then continued, "In the years I've been in the world, and they are many, I've learned quite a few lessons about men and human nature. One of the wisest men I know is a Tennessee mountaineer, with very little book learning, but very wise and well informed. The men of the mining camps used to bring their problems to this man to ask his advice," Harry recalled. "He gave them his attention thoughtfully, talked with them, and when he spoke they were seldom disappointed. Their problems were not always solved," Harry said, "but at least they went away resolved to find the best way out."

"The most honest men I've found out here are the Chinese who work in the mines, and they are mostly Buddhists. The man with the kindest heart, and the most helpful hands, was a Negro," Dan said. "None of these men are what we could call Christians, but they are good men."

"Yes, Doc, one can learn many things from the men who work alongside, be it in the mines, the woods, at sea, or on a farm, if one has the eyes to see and the heart to understand."

Harry and Dan continued their conversation, but I was thinking of a picture from my earlier days, and it made me blush with shame then even more than it did at the time. One of the offices in which I worked employed several young women as stenographers and bookkeepers. When one of the stenographers resigned, another girl was brought in to replace her. Her name was Elizabeth Beasley, and her mother had been a nurse in the superintendent's family. She was one-eighth black.

Miss Beasley was a competent stenographer, her skin was as white as ours; she was pleasant, unassuming, and she tried to be friendly, but in this she was unsuccessful. Her dark eyes and her hair betrayed her black ancestry, and the other women, and some men, muttered among themselves. "She's much too familiar, leaning over our desks to talk to us," and such remarks were made. They also complained that there was a peculiar odour about her. I hadn't noticed these things, perhaps because I had been taught to avoid any form of racial intolerance. However, I did not possess the fortitude necessary to speak up for her, even though I knew we were being unkind to a nice girl who had every right to be there with us. She resigned after one month at the request of the superintendent who had hired her, knowing her to have black ancestry, but he, too, lacked the courage to stand by her. He should have raised her wages (which were less than ours), and told us to mind our own business, or resign. Miss Beasley went into household service.

Noticing my preoccupation, the men asked me why I looked so pensive, but I answered, "How about some coffee? I'm getting hungry!"

It is strange how old ideas and prejudices cling to us despite a changing world, and that some have to die in order to rid themselves of such things.

CHAPTER 16

Equine
Epidemic

D AY AFTER DAY THE CONSTRUCTION WORK went on and the ends of steel crept closer and closer to the completion of the transcontinental railway. Gangs were working from the east, other gangs from the west, and the miles between became a no man's land of activity.

This was a road built by the men's hands as the day of great earth-moving machinery had not yet arrived. Except for a few steam shovels, the digging was done by men with picks and shovels, hand graders and wheelbarrows. Thousands of tons of earth were moved, piled, and graded on the strip laid down by the engineers; men with horses and mules backed and pulled and laboured to make a safe grade to lay track for the heavy trains which would pass over it. Men with shovels dug the drainage ditches, while woodsmen cleared the trees and rocks from the right-of-way. Freight wagons with their six and eight-horse teams, swung into and out of the camp, day after day, the skinners waving their long whips, and waking the echoes with their good-natured singing and shouts.

As the gap narrowed, and the work gangs came closer together, there appeared a noticeable excitement of rivalry, as the grade builders worked like madmen to keep ahead of the track layers. The track layers, in turn, were always trying to catch up with them, to jeer and shout, "Hey, you fellows, get a move on and get to hell out of our way!"

Behind the gangs were the subcontractors, constantly driving, driving for more speed with the work, while they themselves were being pushed by the chief contractors. Still farther in the background was the railway company, determined to have the road finished by spring.

With the bridges completed, the men were now working with pick and shovel, singing their Scandinavian songs in time with the swinging of their powerful arms. The languages of a dozen or more countries were blended in the sounds which filled the bunk houses in the evening, but strangely enough, they were for the most part good friends.

Scarcely a day went by without some casualty on the job, sometimes a fight if tempers became a bit short, and life was a high adventure. A construction job of this dimension, however, drew some undesirable elements into the country, including the camp followers, who fattened on the wages of the workmen. One such person was the former welterweight fighter, Denver Ed Kelly, who had been a champion in his day. After his retirement from the ring, he became a professional gambler, and he arrived in this northern valley to work his magic on the men around the nightly poker tables. Kelly was also a heavy drinker and a bully. Although professional fighters are forbidden by law to use their fists as weapons, Kelly paid no attention to such legalities, and such was his reputation that nobody cared to expose him.

Kelly's partner was a man of his own size, but of a very mild temperament, Jerry Mulvahill. Many wondered why he stayed with Kelly, but Jerry seemed to be something of a lost soul, afraid to leave him because he would then be alone, with nowhere to go. Jerry did all the work around the cabin, waited on Kelly, and cheered for him when he won at poker. He also took a brutal beating from those fighter's hands every time Kelly got drunk.

This had been the pattern of Jerry's life for a long time, and there seemed little chance of changing it. Day after day, however, Jerry built up a slow-burning resentment over his treatment. One night, Kelly went to the camp as usual for his evening's entertainment at the poker table, but Jerry stayed home. He had been badly beaten the night before, and he was nursing his bruises and a gash or two; at the same time his anger had turned into a wild desire for revenge.

After a while, he got up, put on his coat and boots, and reached for his rifle. Then he left the cabin and headed for the bunkhouse to find Kelly.

Climbing onto a stump outside the open window, he looked in and saw his partner intent on his game, just across the room and facing the window. Jerry rested his gun on the windowsill, took careful aim, and fired. Denver Ed Kelly died instantly with a bullet in his brain. Jerry made no effort to escape. All he said was, "I'll never get beaten up again."

He was taken to the end-of-steel at Hazelton, and there he was formally arrested and charged with murder in the first degree. Two men were hired to take him to Prince Rupert for trial.

The early winter snow was falling heavily and when the train was halfway to its destination, it became stalled in the drifts. It was twenty-four hours before the track was cleared, and Jerry had one more day of comparative freedom.

This gave the passengers a chance to hear Jerry's sad story. They saw his bruises and scars and they were convinced that he acted in self-defense. Jerry ended his story of many cruel beatings with the words, "I knew he would kill me sooner or later, maybe the next time he was drunk, and I couldn't take any more."

Most of the men on that train felt that the only justice in the case was Kelly's death. Jerry was like a lost child, and thoughts of either prison or death did not seem to matter to him. He was alone in the world; he had no money, no friends, and nowhere to go.

Jerry was found guilty of premeditated murder, to which he had confessed, and he was sentenced to pay the penalty demanded by law.

The days went by, and the tragedy of Jerry and Kelly was a thing of the past. There was work to be done. Dan and Jim Kerr, the freight superintendent, stopped their horses in front of the office building at the last big camp. They swung out of their saddles and went inside. Tracy, the big, dark buckskin Jim rode, was one of the finest saddle horses in the west. His gait, single-footed, made him very easy to ride, and he had a story all his own. When he was scarcely more than a colt at a farm in Oregon, he was stolen by the famous outlaw of the Pacific Northwest, Harry Tracy, who made a night ride of many miles trying to escape the forces of the law. The lawmen were also looking for the stolen colt, and when Harry abandoned him, and crawled into a field of grain to hide, they found the animal and returned him to his owners. From then on he was called Tracy.

Nobody seemed to know exactly what happened to Tracy for the next few years, but he finally appeared in Pat Burns's corral in Vancouver. The horse was no longer young, but he was one of the best cow horses in the country, and he was used in the packing house yards. With or without a rider, he could cut out any animal, and steer it with his nose right, left, or straight ahead into the chute leading to the slaughter pens. When Burns's company sent a beef drive from the Chilcotin, the foreman chose Tracy for his own mount. He then sold Tracy to the railroad construction company and returned by rail and water to Vancouver. Eventually Tracy became Jim Kerr's mount.

One day Jim said, "He has only one failing. He doesn't like women. You know, my wife can ride almost anything on four legs and wanted to try Tracy. Once when we were at 15 Mile Camp, she persuaded me to change saddles with her for the ride home."

"What happened?" Dan asked. "Did he throw her?"

"No, she's too good a rider to be thrown, but he turned his head when she mounted, took one look at the skirt hanging by his side, and bolted. He clamped his jaw on the bit and ran like a deer. She tried to hold him but she could have saved herself the trouble. He ran the fifteen miles almost without stopping. It was the best ride of her life she said, until she saw the barn door standing open and knew Tracy would make straight for it. She threw herself down alongside his neck and rode right into the barn."

"Where were you all this time? Right behind?"

"Half an hour behind! Didn't even see them after the first couple of miles, because my wife's horse couldn't stand the pace. But she sure lit into me when I got home for not telling her what a tough mouth Tracy had. I just laughed, 'I warned you Tracy didn't like women! Now you'll believe me!' "

" 'I certainly will, and you can have him from now on. If I hadn't noticed that open door, I'd have been decapitated for sure.' "

Dan on "Frank," on road leading out of town.

"Well, there's one thing, Jim, we'll have our horses to ourselves," Dan said, "for Eve certainly can't ride Frank!"

As soon as Dan had collected some necessary supplies from the office building he hurried down to the hospital where, to his surprise, he found the place full of sick horses. Every swing that had gone through for the last two days had left behind one or two horses. A full-scale epidemic of equine typhoid had broken out; Dan would have no more rest while it lasted.

That day he mixed medicine in barrels, and all night long he and his assistants poured medicine down reluctant throats, one quart at a time. He ran out of stimulant drugs and had to use whiskey. When the whiskey ran out, he sent to the nearest blind pig for more. He left his head nurse Bill Gurney in charge of the hospital, with two skinners to help him administer three quarts of medicine, in whiskey bottles, and then he went back to the office for a few hours of rest. When he returned, he found Bill and the skinners singing lustily, their arms around each other, and the horses looking after themselves. Dan was furious and roared at them, "Bill! What's the meaning of this? I left orders that the horses were to be given that whiskey in small doses every half hour, and you drank it yourselves!"

"Och, now, Doc! Sure the horses got some of it. I jist had a few drops once in a while. It was these spalpeens of skinners that drank yer whiskey. The horses are foine. Ye must overlook it this time, Doc."

"Don't let it happen again. I should have known better than to leave you fellows with those bottles. Let's get to work!"

What those men didn't know was that each of those bottles contained only half a bottle of whiskey. The other half was medicine for the horses. The whiskey was just the necessary stimulant. It wouldn't harm them but it might make them sick.

Before the epidemic subsided, hundreds of horses were treated. Every time a swing came in, another batch of horses with hanging heads and wobbling legs was left behind, while the animals which had recovered left to return to work. One horse taken sick was named Skookum, a big raw-boned bay, ugly in line, and mean in disposition. He bit, kicked, and pushed his drivers around, but he was the best worker in the outfit.

The skinner who drove him loved him dearly, as a mother loved a wayward son, and he pleaded, "I don't care if the rest of the swing kick the bucket, but save old Skookum for me, Doc. He's worth it!"

"Of course, Pat, I'll save him if I can, but I think he's too damn mean to die, anyway!"

But Skookum was a very sick horse. Swing after swing came in and went out and still Skookum stood with his head hanging low. It took gallons of medicine and several bottles of whisky before he began to take an interest in life. Then, one morning as Doc came out of the bunkhouse, he met a beaming Pat, "Glory be to God, Doc, what d'ya think? Skookum's goin' to live! Hallelujah!"

"How do you know he's better?" Dan asked.

"Must be, Doc, he took a swipe at me that nearly broke me leg, praise be to the saints!" Just the thought of that vicious kick made a happy man of Pat.

The epidemic was beginning to subside, when Jim received a message one morning that his wife was ill and wanted him to come home. Within minutes Tracy was saddled and Jim was on his way. The gallant horse, now seventeen years old, covered that sixty miles of muddy road, up hill and down in record time. He arrived in town wringing wet and covered with foam. The next morning he was galloping around the pasture like a colt.

Word of this splendid achievement spread throughout the valley, and Tracy was proclaimed the best horse in the West. When Tracy came back to camp, the skinners gathered around and patted the big Roman nose as they led him to the stable, and rubbed him down. He was given an extra feed of oats and covered with a blanket.

Shortly afterwards, Tracy was stricken with typhoid, and there was gloom in all the camps. His great age was against him and he was dying. Jim sat beside him as he lay on the straw, and held the dark head in his arms. With tears shining in his eyes, he looked at Doc and said, "I just can't stand to see him die! Please Doc, put him out of his misery! You know he can't pull through, you said so, and he's dying by inches."

"Yes, I'll take care of it, Jim," Dan said, and taking him by the arm he pushed him gently out of the barn. "You're going to be sick yourself, without sleep for days."

When Jim was out of hearing, Doc put the muzzle of his .44 to the dying horse's head and pulled the trigger. The great horse was at rest.

The skinners turned out that evening and dug Tracy's grave. They wrapped the horse in a new blanket, and buried him in the shade of the nearby trees. When Jim awoke from his sleep of exhaustion he gathered smooth stones, whitewashed them, then formed the name Tracy around the grave. Four stout posts were sunk at the corners and a chain stretched around them. The men said a silent farewell to the horse they all loved and went their way.

The next morning when the camp awakened, a horrible sight met their eyes. In the night the grizzlies had come. The grave was empty, the posts scattered, and nothing but bones and bits and pieces of Tracy remained.

CHAPTER 17

The
Bank
Robbery

THROUGHOUT THE LONG WINTER MONTHS I was lonely. Dan was away most of the time now, as the construction camps had been moved eastward, and the horses and mules were now stabled in the freight camps about fifty miles away. I was not frightened, but just agonizingly lonely.

Then something wonderful happened. Andy Chase, the prospector from Hazelton who owned the sable collie, Pup, came along one day, bringing the golden dog with him. As I greeted him, he said, "You know, Mrs. Doc, ever since you made lap dogs out of our sled team, Pup hasn't been a mite of good to us. Don't get along with the rest of the team at all, thinks he's too good for them mongrels. So, since it's your fault, we figured you would have to take the consequences and look after this here dog. He's yours! That's if you want him." Andy was smiling broadly.

"If I want him!" I almost shouted, "Andy, I'd rather have him than a gold mine. Thanks a million. He can take care of baby and me." My arms were around the Pup's neck and he was nuzzling my face and whimpering joyously.

"That's just it, Ma'am, I gotta warn you that he's never had anything to do with kids, and maybe you better get him used to the baby by degrees. He nearly snapped the arm off a little Native kid once. I think he's scared of them."

Dan was on one his rare visits home at the time, so, Andy stayed for supper, and later I heard him telling Dan, "Pup's feet are too small for the trail; they get all cut up and filled with snow and ice. The other dogs are malamutes, cold feet you know, and snow doesn't cake on them. They travel slower too, and Pup's too eager, stands up on his hind feet and barks, tryin' to hurry them on, then when his feet give out, he's through."

Whatever the reasons for the gift, I was grateful, knowing that the dog would be good company when Margaret and I were alone so much.

At night, Dan and I put a blanket on the floor of the tiny lean-to kitchen we had added to the tent, and Pup settled down as though he knew he had a home with us for the rest of his life.

Margaret slept in a packing box beside us, and it was still early in the morning when I was aroused by the sound of her laughter and squeals. I sat up quickly, but my fears were at once dispelled, as I looked at one of the prettiest pictures in the world.

Pup had crept in when the baby first stirred and there he was, crouched by the box, his big, golden head on her breast. She was pulling at his ears and trying to poke out his eyes. As I watched him, and cautiously pinched Dan to waken him, the dog looked up at me, and I could have sworn he winked. Then his slender forepaw came up across the baby, protectively, and he snuggled closer. Dan and I watched in wonder, thinking of what Andy had said about children. Dan patted the dog's head and smiled. "This is the fierce dog that doesn't like children? If Andy could only see him now!"

From then on, Pup was Margaret's constant companion. When I put her in her carriage for a nap outdoors, he would station himself right beside her, and no one, even our closest friends, dared put a hand on her without hearing his fierce growl. He was a real guardian angel. As soon as Dan left to go back to camp, Pup refused to stay in the kitchen. The moment I put out the light and got into bed, I could hear the soft padding of his feet as he crept in and lay down at the foot of the bed.

The dog kept a strict watch on everyone coming to the tent door, usually reaching it before I did. He chaperoned me most rigidly, and kept the Natives' dogs out of the yard. It was almost unbelievable, but he seemed to have human intelligence, and I got into the habit of talking to him as if he were human.

Unfortunately, some of my neighbours did not consider a dog much use as a chaperone, and they supplemented his efforts, flooding me with attention, and ascertaining that I behaved as a minister's wife should.

I began to feel that Dan was more doctor than husband, and that he loved his sick animals rather more than his family, so I was a bit resentful. Dan, however, had no idea of the surveillance under which I lived, and I was too proud to admit my failure to cope with it. It seemed that a few of the town's older women had taken it upon themselves to monitor the thoughts, words, and deeds of the four or five young wives, and I was the main target because my husband was away from home so much.

If a light burned later than usual in the tent, someone was sure to run in to borrow some coffee or an orange for breakfast, or perhaps a yeast cake to make bread, although any other excuse might serve. One evening, a close neighbour saw a man cross the vacant lot behind the tent, and enter it. I could just imagine how she gloated in anticipation as she promptly knocked at my door. When she entered, her mouth fell open, and words failed her as she found me serving coffee to the wife and two daughters of the invading male. They had spent the evening with me while he attended to certain business affairs, and he was calling to take them home. My neighbour was so embarrassed she forgot what she had intended to borrow, but I cordially invited her to have some coffee with us.

In our canyon town of New Hazelton lived the counterpart of Mrs. Elmer Baxter, my Ontario nemesis. At one time, my newly acquired advisor sent her housekeeper to inform me that my tablecloth had been on the clothesline too long, and that neighbours would think consequently that I was a poor housekeeper. The cloth in question had coffee stains which had only partially washed out, so I had hung the cloth out in the sun and frost in an attempt to bleach the stains away. I left the cloth on the line another week. Shortly afterwards, I did explode in indignation, and avenged myself.

My best friend was Peggy, a young woman my own age, who sang like a lark. Her parents were Roman Catholics, although her husband was a Protestant. She attended our church, often singing for us at evening services. Indeed, her singing was much appreciated, particularly in a place where so few singers were available.

The same woman who had worried about my tablecloth solemnly warned me that it was hardly suitable for the lady of the manse to be so friendly with one who was a Roman Catholic. At first I was stunned by the bigotry and righteous humbug of her remark, but when I did recover my face flamed with anger. "I'm very glad everyone isn't as narrow-minded and bigoted as you are, and that she is kind enough to give us the pleasure of listening to her lovely voice. I suppose when, and if, you get to Heaven, you will insist on the angels signing an affidavit that they are Presbyterians, before you will listen to their singing!" After this belligerent remark, I burst into tears. My caller left the tent in haste without bidding me good-bye, while I wept for an hour. Life seemed a bit too difficult to be borne just then, but there was just one home to which I always fled when I needed a refuge.

This was the home of a Highland Scots woman, Christina Richmond, and her Lowland husband, Jamie. Gossip and Christina were strangers. When one of the local news vendors attempted to tell her some bit of luscious local gossip, she would look them straight in the eyes and say, softly, "You're no sure of what you say, so don't say it. I never listen to gossip!" Very few cared to repeat the experiment. The cold scorn in her dark eyes when rumours circulated around the village was hard to face. Needless to say, I turned to her for comfort many times, and she would laugh gaily and tell me to run along and forget about my troubles.

Those of us who loved music would congregate at her house at least once a week for an evening of singing around the piano. Before we went home, she would serve a delicious lunch, which was a great treat in that land of limited resources. There would be oatcakes as only the Scots make them, delicious cottage cheese, shortbread that melted in one's mouth, and fragrant tea with cream from their own cow. It was a real feast, but it wasn't the piano, nor yet the food that brought us there. It was our gentle, dignified hostess, and her kindly, jovial husband who welcomed us with warmth and sincerity. Christina was beautiful in face and in heart.

To some extent I could understand why the town's good ladies did not approve of me. I did not conform to their idea of a minister's wife. I did not dress like one, nor did I always act like one; I was certainly insufficiently devout. I refused, with Dan's full approval, to take part in the church work, other than playing the organ for the services. He said he was the minister, not his wife. I was young, lighthearted in manner, fond of music and drama, and sometimes resentful enough to say foolish things. Not wicked things, just plain foolish. I may have deserved some of their criticisms, but I hadn't lived long enough to deserve all them. I determined that the next time Dan decided to leave the ministry, I would make him stick to his resolve, or I would leave home, for I had endured enough. (Just here I venture to say that if any minister's wife of my own age should read this, she will understand every word I have said.)

The worry and loneliness had begun to erode my health and suddenly I found myself in bed with a nervous breakdown. The local doctor asked Dan to come home and take care of me. At this point, Dan's work as a veterinary was decreasing as the closing ends of steel from east and west made much of the freighting unnecessary, and horses were being shipped away to other projects. Now it was possible for Dan to remain at home more of the time, with only the occasional trip up the valley. I was happy to have him there, and it was wonderful how quickly I began to recover.

One evening in early November 1913, my first day out of bed, we sat long at the dinner table, talking and drinking coffee. It was such a treat to have somebody to talk to after the long, lonely months when I had only the baby to keep me company, that I felt relaxed and comfortable for the first time.

Suddenly, out of the night came the sound of gunfire, six sharp explosions in quick succession. I did not know that the shots were a distress signal, or I might have been even more alarmed. I began to tremble, and asked, "What's that Dan? Those were shots!"

Dan was worried too, but he did not want to alarm me, so he said, "I expect someone has found a Native dog in his chicken house. There are visiting Native tribes in town and dozens of dogs."

"But six shots. Why?"

"Six dogs, I guess," he replied with a reassuring grin.

I tried to put the sound out of my mind, and had almost stopped shaking when we heard running footsteps on the planks leading to the tent. The door burst open and a young man almost fell through the doorway, shouting, "Doc! They want you to come quick! Bank was held up and one of the boys was shot! He's bleeding bad and they want you to try to stop the blood. The Doctor from the hospital can't get here for a half hour or so!"

Louie gasped this all out in one breath, but after his words Dan leapt to his feet, snatched up his surgical bag, and ran, Louie and I right on his heels. I had forgotten how weak I was until I found myself staggering, and heard Dan say, "Get back into the tent, Eve, and stay there! You're sick, remember."

I remembered it well when I dragged myself back through the doorway and fell into the nearest chair, mumbling to myself, "Just your luck, Eve, something really exciting happens, and you're too weak to see a thing."

I sat quietly for more than half an hour, thinking of finding out what had happened if it killed me, when there was a tap at my door. I called, "Come in. Do come in." I didn't care who it was, it was better than being alone.

It was Ray Fenton, the bank cashier, pale and worried as he dropped on the couch and buried his face in his hands.

"What is it, Ray? Who was hurt?"

"Jock was shot, they don't know how badly yet. Doc had the bleeding stopped before the other Doctor got there, and he said Jock had a bullet in his head. Please, Mrs. MacLean, Doc said you would give me some coffee. I'm all in!"

"Of course, Ray, I think there's still some here in the pot," and I poured him a cup of very strong, black coffee.

He drank it down in one gulp and then said, "You better make some more because the police chief and Hank Little (the bank manager from Hazelton) are coming over to talk to me and I'll need a lot of coffee to keep me going."

"All right, Ray, try and rest until they come and I'll see there is plenty of coffee."

But Ray couldn't rest, instead he paced the floor. I knew he was terribly worried about Jock, so I talked about other things, until I realized he hadn't heard a word I'd said; he muttered to himself, "Why don't they come? They've had plenty of time to get here. If they would only get here and get it over with so I could get down to see Jock!"

There was little official law in the country then. The police were few and far between; some officers hopelessly incompetent to deal with any problems which arose in a new country. Many wrongs and injustices had to be settled by the people themselves, which made it seem like a violent land. It was no more violent than older lands, but where there are many police and courts of law, it is not so close to the people.

I was shaking with weariness by the time the men arrived, but between cups of strong coffee, Ray told his story. "We went to dinner at the usual time and came back in about a half an hour. The back door was locked as usual, but I guess we must have left the bedroom window open because that's how the robbers got in. I unlocked the door and went in and heard a funny, foreign voice saying, 'Get your hands up!'

"I put mine up, but Jock thought it was some of the boys playing a joke on us, so he was slow in obeying. They yelled at him again and he started to raise his hands above his head. I guess one of them must have been nervous because, when Jock's hands were part way up, one of the men shot him, the bullet went into his head close to his eye, and he fell right at my feet. They made me light the lamp and I saw him there, blood all over his face . . . ."

Ray gulped down more coffee while we waited breathlessly to hear more.

"They told me to open the money-box — it was just a small safe — but I didn't have the combination, so they started shooting around my feet to make me hurry and get it open. They were trying to scare me, I guess, but gosh! They didn't need to. I was plenty scared!"

"Go on, what happened then?"

"Well, then, they pulled the safe right out of the vault, one of them pushed

Interior of the Union Bank, New Hazelton.

me into the bedroom and told me not to get up for an hour or I'd get plugged, all the time pointing that nasty gun at me. I don't know exactly how long it was, not more than a minute or two, until I heard them go out of the back door, dragging the box with them. Then I heard Jock's voice. God! It was good to hear him! I was sure he was dead but he was calling, 'Ray! Ray!' I jumped off the bed and ran, without thinking of the guy that was going to plug me if I did.

"They must have left the door open when they went out, and the fresh air revived Jock. I just took one look at him to make sure he was alive, then I ran outside and fired the six shots as a distress signal."

"Didn't you see anyone around when you ran out?"

"Not a soul. It's only a couple of jumps into the bush and they must have gotten there before I ran out."

Again the coffee pot was passed around and emptied, so I went into the kitchen to make more. I was shaking with fear and excitement while the questioning went on.

"How long was it before your signal was answered?"

"Just a minute or two. It seemed a very short time before two or three fellows ran over to see what was wrong. We picked Jock up and carried him into MacLeod's house across the street. Louie ran up for the Doc, while I telephoned the hospital."

Ray again buried his face in his hands and the others were silent. When they left a few minutes later, I went with them to the house where the wounded boy was now in the hands of two doctors from the hospital, with Dan assisting them as they probed for the bullet. So many people had gathered by this time that the kitchen and porch were overflowing; all were waiting anxiously to hear the verdict, whether it would be life or death for the victim. Jock was only nineteen, a young Scots lad who had never been away from home until he had come to work in the New Hazelton bank. He was liked by everyone and it was an anxious crowd that milled around waiting for news of him. After a time the doctor came out. "Well, my friends, I think the boy will pull through" he said, "but we can't take the bullet out before having him x-rayed. He's sleeping now, with a morphine injection, so you had better all go home."

"Home, nothin'," cried an excited voice. "We're goin' after them bandits and string 'em up!" There was a roar of approval from the crowd.

One of the older men spoke then, "There'll be no posse sent out tonight, boys. In this bright moonlight we'd be too much of a target for those boys in the bush. Put away your guns, wait till daylight, when the police arrive."

"Police! One policeman! And he don't know anything about this country. Lot of good he'll be!"

"Well, wait till morning, anyway, and maybe we can catch the gang before they get too far down river." And so it was decided, and the crowd went home. I didn't get away quite quickly enough. I was waiting to see Dan, who seemed to have disappeared.

Knowing him as I did, I was not sure that he might have appointed himself a posse of one to go after the bank robbers, so I was really in a panic. The doctor who had allowed me to get out of bed for the first time that day, saw me and pounced. "What in the world are you doing here? Where's your husband?

What is he thinking of to let you out of the house?"

"I don't know where he is and no one else seems to either." My voice was shaking, not to mention my knees. The doctor laughed, "He's not out chasing bandits, you can be sure, so don't worry about him. Now you go along and get back to bed."

I went home as ordered, but I didn't go to bed. It was another hour before Dan appeared. My temper had overcome my fear by this time, and I was very angry when he strolled in and announced nonchalantly that he had been called away to see a sick horse. "Sorry to leave you for so long, Eve, but I knew someone would tell you where I was."

"How could they? No one knew where you were, and I was so frightened I could hardly walk home. The doctor was angry and said I might have to stay in bed another week."

Next morning, the posses went out, one group going up river while the other group went down river, each searching the woods for any sign of the gang. Those who went westward down river soon found evidence of an overnight camp. The money box lay there broken and empty. The posse hurried after the robbers, searching for them all day, but the gang seemed to have disappeared completely.

The sum total of this robbery was a young man's death, for Jock failed to recover from his wound, while the bank lost more than $16,000 — quite a sum in those days, even for the Union Bank of Canada.

CHAPTER 18

A Visit
to
Duncan Ross
Tunnel

I<small>T WAS WINTER BEFORE I HAD ENTIRELY RECOVERED</small> from my
relapse the night of the bank robbery. Margaret spent her days under the
supervision of one or another of my close friends, and she seemed to thrive on
it. The guardian she seemed to like most was Mary Wilson, my laundress from
the Hagwilget village. Mary was a tall, well-formed woman, although she was
quite stout. Her hair and eyes were shiny black, her face eager and kindly. She
was a Kispiox woman, but lived in the Carrier village of Hagwilget, as her
husband was himself a Carrier.

One day, she sat resting after the washing was finished, holding Margaret
on her knee, while I made lunch. She told me of the death of the husband of
one of her friends in Kispiox. He had disappeared while he was fishing in the
Skeena. His body had just been found some miles down river, washed up on
shore. Mary was smiling mischievously as she said, "I think, Mrs. Doc, maybe
his wife push him in river when he was fishing."

"Oh, Mary! You shouldn't say a thing like that! Why should she?"

"Jacob, he very bad husband. He fish all time, but no catch fish, he too lazy
to pull um in. He never help Hannah like my Abraham help me. Many times
my husband carry water for me when I wash for white ladies. Jacob never do
anything, just lie around, and let Hannah do work. All he do is make babies,

one every year, and they have big family maybe eleven, twelve children. Yah, I think she push him in."

The smug smile on Mary's face fascinated me, but I didn't dare laugh. "You mustn't say things like that, Mary. Maybe the police will hear about it, and then what would Hannah do?"

"Policeman never know for sure, nobody see, nobody know anything."

Thinking it over, and remembering the hordes of little children I had seen on the reservation, I decided my sympathy was for Hannah. After all, women must stand together, so I did not mention Mary's idea to anyone.

Now that trains were running from the coast to New Hazelton, our mail arrived regularly, and just before Christmas I received a letter from my old friend, Marie. She wrote, "You will notice from the postmark that I am now in Vancouver. So many things have happened since I left Hazelton that I scarcely know where to start. Hank and I opened a cafe in Prince Rupert, but it didn't do very well as so many of the mines have closed down. Then Hank received a letter from his mother in Ontario, asking him to come home. I didn't mention this to you before, but Hank's mother is a cousin of Harry Davies. Before he died, Harry made a will leaving everything he had to me. Hank's mother was very angry about it, as she was his nearest relative in this country, and she had expected to inherit his mine. That is why they sent for Hank to come home.

"I have not seen him since he left. Two months afterward a lawyer sent me divorce papers to sign, but, instead, I wrote asking for an explanation. Hank then wrote that his father was dead, and now that his mother was alone, he could not leave her. He was sure I would be all right since Harry had provided for me, and I would be better off without him. This is how he put it, 'Of course I had to tell them that you had been a dancehall girl in the Yukon, and now that I am home again, I can see that it would not work, you and me, I mean. My father was a rich man and I am sure you would not be happy living among our friends. Please be a good girl and sign the papers.' After that, there didn't seem to be anything else to do, so I signed them and sent them back. I guess I am better off without him, but I do miss him, and I loved him, even though I knew he was very weak in character.

"Harry Davies wrote that he was leaving me his money because he knew Hank would not stay with me long, and he didn't want me to be left with nothing. It seems he knew the breed better than I did! I shall try to buy a rooming house here in Vancouver with the money Harry left me, and if ever you come down I will be very happy to have you stay with me. I am trying to forget everything that has happened and make a new life for myself. I hope the baby is well and that you and Doc are as happy as ever!"

When I finished reading I felt sick with disgust. What made a man treat a woman like Marie in this cruel fashion? Whatever her experiences in the Yukon, they were no different from his. When I remembered all Marie's kindnesses to me, and all the trouble she had endured in her early life, I was happy at her decision to make a new life for herself, completely different and among strangers. I wished her the very best of fortune in her undertaking.

I put the letter back into the envelope slowly. I was sorry for Marie, and furious with Hank, although I was sure she was much better off without him, with all his money. He had to inherit it, he couldn't have made it. I sat down and answered Marie's letter at once, and told her I would certainly see her if the trip to Vancouver ever materialized.

It had been quite a shock to us when old Harry died. We had grown very fond of him, knowing his kindness, his integrity, and wisdom. He asked for Dan and when the doctor sent word that Harry was failing fast, Dan went to see his old friend at once. The poor old fellow had a weak heart and a severe attack of bronchitis had been too much for it. Dan stayed the night with Harry, and about 10:00 the next morning, the old man had put out his hand, and Dan held it until Harry passed away a few minutes later.

We were surprised to hear that he was related to Hank Williams, but happy to know that he had been so good to Marie. She was much better clay than Hank ever would be, and his mother's disapproval meant nothing to any of us.

The letter depressed me somewhat, and Dan, noticing my glumness, suggested that what I needed was a change.

"You know Eve, there's only one big construction camp left now, and I think we should pay them a visit. We'll take the little organ and you can give the boys some music. What do you say?"

"I say yes by all means, let's go someplace."

Dan borrowed a horse and, using Frank as a mate, he hitched the two to a cutter for the drive. Frank had never worn harness before, as far as we knew, and was quite indignant about it. Being an outlaw, even with a saddle on, he certainly gave us a merry ride up those twenty odd miles to the Duncan Ross Tunnel Camp. We arrived just in time for supper and ate a hearty meal in the cook house as soon as we were warm and rested. We were to stay the night in the superintendent's cabin, as he was away on business. About eight o'clock we went down to the big dining room, which had been cleared for the occasion, and found about two hundred men crowded in, sitting on benches, stools, and on the tables along the walls.

As usual, I played the little organ and sang until I was exhausted. The men sang with me, any song they knew, but I couldn't find anyone who would sing a solo, until someone remembered that one of the bookkeepers, John McLeod, had been a concert singer in Scotland before coming to Canada, so he was immediately conscripted. Unwilling at first, he was persuaded by a couple of drinks of his favourite brand of inspiration, and then he gave us a recital. He had a beautiful tenor voice, which we all enjoyed, but once he had started, he couldn't be stopped. When he finished from sheer exhaustion, everyone had gone except the cook, and he was asleep in his bunk.

We had to get up very early the next morning if we expected to have any breakfast, and it seemed as though we had scarcely fallen asleep when we were awakened by the cook's voice shouting, "Come and get it." We lost no time answering the summons.

After breakfast we decided to explore the Duncan Ross Tunnel. The first half of the tunnel extended through a gravely hill, and this part was open from floor to roof, but the last one hundred yards had only a heading through, so, though we started out walking, when we came to the second half Dan said, "Let's climb up and go right through to the other end. We can crawl, and then you'll be the first woman through the tunnel." Quite a distinction, I thought.

"Let's!" I replied. Away we went on our hands and knees. What a crawl! When we emerged from the other end into the sunlight, I was dirt-covered from head to foot, my knees were scratched, and my heart was pounding from wondering what would happen if the tunnel caved in. I didn't know whether I had been adventurous or just plain foolish. However, I was the first woman to go through the tunnel.

Dan brought me home that day, but had to return to the camp immediately as there were several horses needing attention. A six-horse swing had gone over a bank with its freight wagon and every horse had been cut somewhere before the men were able to release them and get them back to the road. It was a week before Dan was able to leave them, and he had several stories to tell when he came home.

One freight swing had taken on a new driver named Mack, a Metis. As Mack had been with the company only a short time, the other skinners were not familiar with his habits. Every evening when the teams pulled into camp, Mack would take a sniff of the white stuff which turns men into supermen, and become immediately belligerent.

One night he took his usual sniff and walked into the cook house just ahead of a small man called Scotty, from Glasgow. As Scotty stepped inside the door, Mack turned and swung a right-hand blow to Scotty's chin, knocking him cold. The next morning Scotty took his swing out as usual but he was nursing more than a sore jaw. He was angrier than he had ever been before.

When the swings returned to camp that night and Mack went through his usual procedure, Scotty, about half Mack's size, stepped up on a bench, snatching up a stove lid in passing. When Mack turned toward him, he cut a biscuit out of the big man's scalp as neatly as you please. This time it was Mack who passed out. When questioned about the affair, Scotty said indignantly, "I wasna' goin' to let the beeg stiff hit me fairst again!"

Mack recovered, but he had a very sore head for quite a while.

Dan had another story for me which was quite different, and while I had laughed about the story of the stove lid, this one made me feel more like crying.

Black Jack MacDonell's Roadhouse, near Moricetown, where Scotty avenged himself.

"Do you remember me telling you about Popcorn Kate's roadhouse? The one we all try to miss at mealtimes?"

"You mean the woman who makes vegetable soup with bacon rinds and beet tops and all?"

"And when it's chicken soup we know, because there are always some feathers to prove it. When I was going back to the camp by stage last week there was a stranger, a young chap, about twenty, I think, going along. None of the other four men or myself had ever seen him before and we wondered what he could be doing up here. A couple of the others had been drinking enough to make them very talkative, and we were all telling the driver to hurry up and get up past Kate's before dinner time. One fellow said, 'It's like a game of hopscotch we play when we're freightin', tryin' to stop before we get there, or after we're past, to get a meal.' The other one turned to the stranger, 'Ever been up this way before, lad? If ye haven't ye should try one of Popcorn's dinners. It 'ud be an experience ye'd never forget.'

'No, I haven't been this way before. How far is it to her place?'

'Just up ahead. Yes, sir, ye can get anything at all up at Kate's place, eatin', drinkin', or anything else,' and the skinners went on to add a few more unflattering details. The boy said nothing but something in his face made me ask, 'You don't know Kate, do you?'

'Yes, I know her,' he said, looking at our astonished faces, and added, 'she's my mother.'"

"I assure you, Eve," my husband continued, "we didn't do any more talking until the boy climbed down at the roadhouse. It was quite a shock!"

"Oh, the poor boy! I wonder if he knew the kind of place she was running?"

"I don't think so, from the look on his face when we were talking. I felt sick when I remembered our conversation."

There were times when I had to think very hard about the kind hearts to be found in that great country, to forget about all the degradation which had crept in from the outside world. The law didn't mean much up there; policemen not only frequented the blind pigs and dens of vice, it was said they owned some of them. One place, not far from a railroad camp, was noted for its expert rolling of the men after payday. Scotty, the Glasgow skinner, had lost every cent of his month's wages the only time he went there. He solemnly swore that the only person in the room when he lost consciousness was a policeman. As a consequence, he wasn't very fond of policemen.

CHAPTER 19

Return Engagement at the Bank

T HE GAP BETWEEN THE ENDS OF STEEL WAS CLOSING fast as construction of the railway neared completion. Men were being laid off every week, and the banks were full of money for the final payday. Then the day arrived when the Grand Trunk Pacific transcontinental railway was an accomplished fact.

The morning of April 7, 1914, was clear and sunny, and in the town of New Hazelton great excitement abounded as this was the day the last spike would be driven and the line would be in operation across Canada, from sea to sea. Politicians and railway directors were coming from all parts of Western Canada to be present at the ceremony. Some were already in town doing a little electioneering for the coming test of government. Among them was John Oliver, soon to be British Columbia's premier, and several of his party. The stage was set for the second bank robbery, but this time a very different story would be told.

After the robbery in November 1913, another attempt was to be expected, as the men managed to escape easily with their booty on that occasion. Since then, the bank had installed a time lock on its vault, so the repeat performance would have to take place in daylight.

It was washday at our place, Mary had just arrived, and she was busy

Newly opened railway station at New Hazelton (circa 1913).

arranging her tubs for the day's work. Dan was at home and had picked up a
pail to water the saddle horses which were stabled nearby. In the intersection
of Pugsley Street and Tenth Avenue stood a large boulder of silver ore rock on
a solid wooden base, which had been presented to the town by the Silver
Standard Mining Company. On either side of the rock were the town pump
and the fire alarm triangle. Our tent was a half block away on Tenth Avenue,
while the bank was about the same distance along Pugsley Street.

The corner lot between the intersection and the bank was partially cleared,
leaving a tangle of stumps and downed trees. Dan was about halfway to the
pump when he heard gunshots and saw Barrie Tatchell, the bank manager,
running across the vacant lot, leaping logs, dodging stumps, and shouting.
"Another hold-up, Doc. Get your gun!"

Down went the pail in the middle of the road and the two men raced to
the tent. They dashed through the doorway; Dan tossed his .44 Colt six-
shooter to Barrie, and seized his Lee Enfield army rifle from the wall where it
hung. Before more than a few seconds had elapsed they were running back
down the street. Dropping flat on the ground behind the ore pile, they turned

The Union Bank, New Hazelton, the site of the Bank Robberies.

their guns on the bank doorway where a man with a rifle was clearing the streets with a hail of bullets. It was fortunate there were few people in that end of the town, as many of the businesses had moved east to the site of the new railway station. This was the morning the train was due from the west, and a crowd was always on hand to greet it. The bullets from the bank doorway had made it necessary for those nearby to take cover.

I was terrified, because nobody had told me what was happening, and with a panic-stricken look at Mary and the baby, I too went outside saying, "Never mind the washing, Mary, just look after the baby."

I heard Dan shout, "Get back into the tent, Eve," but of course I didn't obey. I climbed up on a fallen tree across the street from the tent, hoping to find out what it was all about. I could only see the men behind the rock and hear bullets whizzing (I thought), but the roar of the rifles was not imagination, and it filled me with a terrible fear for the boys in the bank where guns were popping steadily.

Suddenly, the man in the bank's doorway found he could no longer handle the situation, and he called to the others to come to his aid. As they came, emptying their guns at the ore pile, they fell; the first two died instantly while the third was fatally wounded.

Then I saw Dan rise to his feet and, with a lightning spurt, he ran across the remaining half of the street to the shelter of the general store, disappearing through its doorway. He had risked the short run, he later told me, because he needed more ammunition; his gun had not been fully loaded, and it was now empty. When I saw him dodging the bullets, I closed my eyes, but I had not counted on the speed of those long legs. Even a movie camera would scarcely have caught him, except as a blur. He ran into the store, caught the new box of shells which Hughie Richmond threw to him, then disappeared around the building to the back corner, almost exactly across from the bank.

The robbers must have been expecting him because, as he cautiously looked around the corner, a rifle bullet chipped the wall right above him.

Tatchell was still behind the ore pile, but was joined almost at once by Arizona Smith, whose lodging house was a short distance away. Smith ran up the middle of the street, and, being a former baseball player, he slid on his stomach the last ten feet to base beside Tatchell, and turned his shotgun on the general confusion in the direction of the bank. The four men remaining were making desperate efforts to reach the shelter of the woods on the other side of the bank. They had not had time to reload their guns, and their only hope was to get away. There was a horse tied to a tree beside the road, waiting his turn at the blacksmith shop a few yards further along. The bandits tried to get one of their wounded on its back, but they had to abandon that idea, so they left the horse standing where he gave some them protection as they fled into the woods, all of them wounded.

Quiet fell over the street scene as there was no hurry now. Their wounds would not permit the four to travel, and now it was just a matter of going down into the woods to gather them in. At least the townsmen hoped so.

When the bank had opened that morning, several customers had arrived to make their usual deposits from the previous day's business. The cashier, Robert

Bishop, who had missed the first robbery because he was on vacation at the time, had just taken a small box of money from the vault to begin the day's work. The manager, who alone knew the combination of the safe, had not yet arrived at the bank. Fenton, a veteran of the first robbery, was there, busy with his books.

About 10:30, seven men, all wearing long raincoats, had walked abreast up the street from the direction of the railway tracks. They were not noticed particularly as the town was swarming with groups of men waiting for the train to take them out of the country. The seven walked directly to the bank door, six of them entering, while the seventh stood in the doorway with a rifle, which he had drawn from under his long coat. He began at once to shoot up and down the street to discourage any interference. Needless to say, the street was immediately cleared.

Inside the bank, the bandits relieved the customers of their deposits at gun point; Bishop was ordered in the same manner to "Hand over the money," — for the second time those words had been heard in five months. He was then ordered to open the safe, although he was unable to do so until the manager's arrival.

Tatchell was asked later how he managed to escape. He responded, "I wasn't in the bank, I was standing outside between the crossed ends of the logs talking to a fellow when I heard the first shots. I tried to go inside and was met by the man in the doorway, who stuck a gun in my face. I ducked back behind the log ends and ran around behind the bank, and across towards Doc's place. I knew he would help, that he had guns and knew how to use them. Lord! I was glad to see him!"

"So that's how it was!" Dan marvelled. "You were travelling across that lot so fast I don't think a bullet could have caught you if he had sent one after you!"

Indelibly written on the minds of the people of New Hazelton was the brutal murder of Jock McQueen by the same men, or so everyone believed. Jock's death had occurred shortly before this, and the shots heard inside the bank made both Dan and Tatchell terribly afraid there might be more deaths. The bandits were careful this time to avoid murder charges as well as robbery.

I had been standing on that log, to which my feet seemed to be glued, from first to last of the shooting, and I thought my heart would burst with fear. I had seen two of the men who were trying to escape into the woods helping each other climb over a log. Another shot was fired, and both fell to the ground. I saw them rise cautiously and crawl into the woods. I wished I had a gun just then, because I could see them plainly, one of them carrying the bag containing the money stolen from the bank, an amount reported to be about $900.00. Since I had never fired a gun in my life, and couldn't have hit them anyway, my wish was foolish, but I had been willing to try. With the guns once more silent, I jumped to the ground and ran across to the tent, expecting to find Mary badly alarmed. Instead she was calmly proceeding with the washing, while the baby was sitting on the floor playing with her toys. Mary looked up and said calmly, "What happened, Mrs. Doc, I heard many people shoot?"

She hadn't even opened the door to see what was happening.

Seeing Mary and Margaret contented and unconcerned, I walked down the street to join the crowd which had gathered beside the bank. By this time almost the whole town was there, the office staff, visiting politicians, even the policeman, who had not shown himself before. Groups of men were discussing the best way to capture and bring back the rest of the bandits. The wives were there, too, and they were frightened but resolute. When I looked for Dan, I couldn't see him anywhere.

There was a man in town named Nelson, who did odd jobs, splitting wood, carrying water, and other necessary work. He was a Scandinavian, and most people thought he was half-witted. After that day, I knew better, because in that whole group of people he was the only one who understood the look of horror in my eyes, not being able to ask the question which trembled on my lips. He looked at me, came over, and laying his work-roughened hand on my arm, he said quietly, "Doc's all right, ma'am, wasn't hurt at all! He's over back of the bank gettin' a bunch of the fellers together to go down into the woods. Don't you worry none!"

I wanted to throw my arms around his neck, but that might have frightened him out of the rest of his wits.

I walked slowly past the men who lay still and no longer dangerous, their guns empty and still warm, to find Dan talking to a small group of men who were known to be capable of taking care of themselves. The only policeman in town was a young man, in office for the first time; although he was a pleasant fellow, he was a better hockey player than a policeman. He had asked Dan to take charge of the search in the woods, admitting that he had neither the courage nor the experience to do it.

The six chosen men divided into pairs and walked silently into the left, right, and centre of the deep woods, determined to bring out the four men who were in there hiding. As Dan disappeared, I went back to the store and Christina, who was still shaken from her own experience.

As the first shots were heard, Christina, who lived almost directly across the street from the bank, opened her front door, expecting to see hawks flying, or Native dogs running for their lives. The answer came immediately as a bullet hissed through the wall just above her head, and into her daughter's bedroom, shattering the dresser mirror. Fortunately, her daughter was not in the room, for she might easily have been killed. Christina fled through the back door into the shelter of her husband's store.

We waited breathlessly for the men to return after hearing a couple of shots down in the woods. The waiting was hard to bear but we were not entirely without a diversion to break the suspense.

Down the road from Old Hazelton came a horse and rider at full speed. Then, carefully skirting the bodies on the street, he rode right into the blacksmith shop a little beyond, jumped down, and cautiously closed the doors. The blacksmith had just returned to his shop, and gazed at the young man with open-mouthed wonder as he pulled a pearl-handled revolver from his pocket and demanded in a loud voice, "Now. Where are they?"

George Wall, the blacksmith, exploded in sudden laughter and asked him, "Who are you looking for?"

"The bandits of course, the ones who were holding up the bank!"

"Well, you damn near ran over some of them when you rode down the street, but the live ones are down in the woods waiting to be grabbed and brought back. Want to go down?"

The first to fall. *(British Columbia Archives and Records Service #29594)*.

The young man shuddered and, replacing the gun in his pocket, he tiptoed out of the shop and walked back to where the men were lying. He noticed someone was about to take some pictures, so he went over, placed his foot on the chest of one of the prostate victims, and turned a stern face toward the camera. When he had been hastily removed, the pictures were taken.

In the meantime, Fenton who was still in the bank assessing the damage, decided to join the crowd outside, and walked slowly toward the door. One townsman, who had been late in arriving on the scene and hadn't heard the latest bulletins, crouched behind a stump several yards away and raised his shotgun. He aimed at what he thought must be one of the bandits, and sent a full charge of buckshot through the window. As the doctor later picked buckshot and glass out of his shoulder, Fenton said ruefully, "It wasn't enough to have those bandits scare me almost to death, but I have to be shot by one of my friends!"

Incidents such as these took our minds off the men in the woods, at least for the moment, but again we waited, all eyes fixed on the edge of the forest. At last we saw them emerging as one group, bringing a wounded man with them. They came straight to the bank, and were followed almost immediately by others of the searchers, with the fifth man. The doctors from the hospital had arrived, and the two bandits were turned over to them for examination before they were taken to the hospital.

The chief of police from Old Hazelton had also arrived, and when the men went into the bank they found him on his hands and knees in front of the safe, apparently looking for spent shells. In reply to their derisive remarks he told them as he rose to his feet, stiff with dignity, "These men are evidently dangerous criminals, and I must have positive proof of their guilt."

The shouts of laughter which followed his words must have been hard to bear. When you consider that two men lay dead, one dying, two more in custody, all with empty guns still smelling of fresh gunfire; every tree, log, and door jamb near the bank inlaid with lead, and that several people were eye-witnesses to the affray, he sounded quite ridiculous. He had been trained in police work in his native city of London, and had not been in British

New Hazelton citizens watch two wounded bandits get a ride to jail. *(British Columbia Archives and Records Service #52248).*

Corpses lie on the sidewalk after the bank robbery. *(Btitish Columbia Archives and Records Service #29588)*

Columbia's north quite long enough to be familiar with either the country or the people.

Five men were now accounted for, but numbers six and seven were still at large. They told me that Dan and another man were down watching the railway track, as it was expected the bandits would try to cross over into the dense forest on the other side. The men of the posse were grim-faced in their laughter. None had stopped for food, and they were tired as well as hungry and angry.

About four that afternoon, Dan and his partner were concealed, as much as they could be on the right-of-way, watching every movement of any kind. Then Dan saw a glint of sun shining on the barrel of a rifle which was aimed straight at them, about a hundred yards away. He raised the Lee Enfield and shot quickly. The rifle disappeared, and they went down and picked up number six. He was badly wounded, with a bullet through his left hand and right shoulder, and he was bleeding profusely. After bandaging him with handkerchiefs and belts, Dan brought him back to the bank, leaving his partner to watch for the last of the seven. Dan's partner, however, followed him right back, and the seventh man crossed the track to what he hoped was safety.

After giving first aid and bandages, the cavalcade left with the doctors for the hospital where the dead men were placed in the morgue and the others in a ward under the guard of our policeman who was less fearful of the bandits now they were incapacitated.

The townsmen were certain that the seventh man would head either up or down the Bulkley River, so they told the chief of police where they thought he might be found. One old-timer heard them and snorted, "He ain't lost no bandit!"

The posse, however, felt they had done all they could and the men decided to head for home. Just then a Native from Hagwilget rode up on a steaming pony and shouted "White man sit on bank of creek outside village, wash leg in water. I come quick to tell you — maybe he one of bad men who shoot!"

"What did he look like, Isaac, old man or young?"

"Big man. Red hair. How old I not know."

Dan and Jim Kerr at once forgot their resolution to let the police handle the seventh man and they hastily saddled their horses. As they mounted, intending to lose no time, they were stopped by the government agent from Old Hazelton, who had just arrived. He said sternly, "Look here, you two, where do you think you're going? You can't do things like this, you're not properly sworn in and you have no a license to carry those guns."

Dan and Jim looked at each other, and then at the agent.

"What do you think, Jim?"

Jim's reply must have burned the agent's ears, but it brought a grin to the faces of the men gathered around them. They remembered the early hours of the day and wondered what might have happened if there had not been men with guns who knew how to use them expertly. Those bandits did not intend to stop at robbing the bank, they were prepared to lay long siege to the whole town. Since not only Dan and Jim, but many other men had worn guns when necessary ever since coming to the country, the official order seemed not only unjust, but plain stupid.

"Very well," Dan said, "go get him yourself!" The two men dismounted and put the horses back in the stable.

The seventh man was never captured, although it became known that he was an American, and that he carried the money taken from the bank.

The day's excitement was beginning to subside, and I walked slowly home to the tent. I knew Dan must be feeling very, very low, because of his feeling of responsibility for the bandit's death. He had not been trying to save the bank's money, but he had remembered Jock and his cruel death. The way in which the bandits had been shooting up and down the street, and the marks of many bullets on the ore pile gave evidence that it had been a matter of kill or be killed. Dan had no choice other than take part in the action against the robbers because he was the only man close at hand who had a rifle and knew how to use it.

Then, for the first time in about four hours, I saw Dan coming up the street. All the repressed fear of that dreadful day came flooding over me, and I started weeping uncontrollably. A quick step towards me, and Mary's arms were around me. She held me closely in her warm arms and said softly, "Please, Mrs. Doc, you not cry so hard. You think of little baby you carry, maybe you hurt it." I stopped my hysterical sobbing immediately, and she went on, "Everybody all right now, Doc is home."

Then Dan came in, and when my eyes were dried he said, "Christina says she will take care of Margaret while I take you down to the hotel for supper. Hurry up and get dressed, because I'm awfully hungry!"

When he had left to take Margaret down to Christina I tried to thank Mary for all her care and loving kindness, but she laughed and said, "I like babies, Mrs. Doc, and it's nice to take care of just one baby. I have five kids and they make so much noise, I go crazy. Now you take care of yourself and no more cry. Promise!"

As I watched her walk straight and tall down the street, I couldn't help thinking what a world of knowledge and perception she possessed, knowing

Dan beside the Silver Ore Rock in Old Hazelton, which features prominently in the bank robbery.

the one thing that would stop my crying. I envied her calmness, her poise, and most of all her kind heart. She was proud of her husband, a small man who scarcely reached her shoulder and who, she claimed, was very kind to her, because he sometimes carried water for her when she went to wash clothes for white women.

Comparing Mary with the type of woman who had laughed at Mr. Coppermines, and had refused to share his long weary summers in the northern mines, I wondered why so many people consider it an honour to be whites, rather than Native.

I had accumulated a good deal of experience in that long, frightening day, and when I hurried out to meet Dan I was completely exhausted and subdued.

I slipped my hand into his pocket as we walked along. I felt the need to touch him but I was sure he would think it undignified to walk hand in hand.

My fingers touched a fragment of stone and I drew it out to see what it was. It was a sliver of ore-filled rock. Silver ore!

"Where did this come from Dan? Prospecting?"

"Not exactly," he replied. "That fellow in the bank door this morning made me a present of it as he chopped it off just above my head so close it landed in my Stetson brim. Thought I'd keep it as a souvenir."

I dropped it back into his pocket without a word. I couldn't speak just then because of a lump in my throat. Dan took my hand and tucked it under his arm. He seemed to feel the need of contact too.

The hotel was down close to the station, nearly a half-mile from the older part of town. It seemed strange that the station was built in a place so inaccessible to the existing village. Later, I learned that this procedure was followed all the way along the line, and that all the established towns were bypassed, because, in the eyes of the railroad barons, the wrong people owned the land on which the towns were built. No self-respecting railroad company officials could disappoint their friends who had bought property with the understanding that a station would be built adjacent to their land.

Events moved swiftly for the next few days although, as we expected, the police were unable to find the seventh man.

As the inquiries proceeded, the bandits were identified as a group who had been living for several days in a cabin about a hundred yards from the bank. Every available cabin was filled with men, so they attracted no attention whatever, except for the tall man with red hair. The hotel bartender noted that the fugitive was evidently an American, that he looked like one, and that he had no foreign accent, as the others had.

Listening to the conversation, I suddenly gasped and Dan asked what was the matter.

"I just thought of something awful!" I said. "Do you remember when I went down for the milk the night before the robbery? It was later than usual and almost dark. I met those very same seven men! They were coming back from the hotel, and they were all drunk, rolling along, and singing at the tops of their voices. It was right in that narrow place by the cutbank, and the sidewalk is only two planks wide. When they saw me, the rest of the men stepped off into the roadway, but the big fellow with the red hair stayed on, until he was right in front of me. One of the others grabbed him by the tail of his raincoat and pulled him off, saying, 'Get out of the lady's way, ya big bum!' and the redhead fell backwards and sat down in the mud. I kept right on going but I was laughing as hard as they were. Dear God, I'm glad I didn't know I was going to see them all shot up!"

Dan looked slightly pale, but all he said was, "You sure manage to get right in the middle of things, don't you Eve!"

Remembering those laughing, singing men, who were so polite to me a few hours before, made the ghastly slaughter of the next morning seem more gruesome than ever.

As soon as the three prisoners in the hospital had recovered sufficiently to appear, Judge Young arrived from Prince Rupert to preside at the trial. Every one of the robbers had been found wearing a belt filled with ammunition, cartridges which held soft-nosed bullets, each with a deep crosscut on the end. Men who use "dum dums" are not only gunmen, they are killers, so it was fortunate that few people were in that end of town at the time of the bank robbery.

The judge found the prisoners guilty of armed robbery with intent to kill, and he sentenced them to twenty years in the provincial penitentiary. Having proved that these were the same men who committed the robbery in November 1913, and thinking of the boy who lost his life, the judge felt it his duty to give them the maximum sentence.

CHAPTER 20

The Avenging Brother Visits

I KNEW I HAD TO PUT THE AFFAIR out of my mind as quickly as possible for the sake of my new baby which was due in September. Fortunately, we were busy, as we were at last moving out of the tent into a roomy, comfortable log cabin. It had deep window ledges, a door on the bedroom, and there was a bathroom in which we found a full-length tub, lined with tin. What a luxury after washtubs!

At last it was warm, lovely summer, and I was beginning to forget the horror of April. Then, one evening in June, my friend Peggy asked me to go for a walk with her. We strolled along, sniffing the wild-rose-scented air, happy and content. Our calm, however, was suddenly shattered when Red McDougall came running toward us, waving a paper and saying, "I got a message for Doc from the police station." I told him Dan was at home, and asked what had happened this time. He handed me a paper on which was written:

"Gang heading for New Hazelton to clean up on those responsible for the shooting of men in bank hold-up. Led by brother of Marko and de-scribed as follows: age thirty years, weight up to two hundred pounds, dark complexion, brown suit of clothes, has false mustache which he may be wearing. Has a gun, a belt, has come here with the intention of getting revenge on the men who participated in bank robbery April 7, 1914."

I think my heart stopped beating for a while, but Peggy took me gently by the arm and told Red, "We'd better get this message to Dan. Thanks, Red, we'll look after it for you."

I couldn't speak on the way home, but my friend knew how severe this new shock had been because I was trembling violently. Peggy stayed with me while Dan went down to the police station to confer with the constable. This time, Dan allowed himself to be sworn in as a special deputy, as the time might come when he would need legal authority as well as a gun.

The supplementary letter, which arrived from the Vancouver police, said an informer had told them the gang was talking mostly about a tall priest with curly hair. That almost finished me, but Dan took the news calmly and merely said, "They will need to be more accurate in their shooting than the others were if they plan to shoot me."

This was said for my benefit, but the constable warned him, "they may shoot from behind a tree or through your window at night. From now on pull down your blinds before you light a lamp. That's an order!"

Once again the old terror swept over me. Dan tried to prevent me from becoming too badly frightened, but I was in no state to be comforted. I moved through the days and nights with barely breathing, mainly fighting to remain calm for the baby's sake, but in an agony of fear for Dan.

Everyone was on the alert as the days went slowly by, waiting for the man of vengeance to appear. Then, one day, the gang leader, brother of one of the men who died on the street in front of the bank, arrived in town.

Early that afternoon Dan left the house and walked down the road leading to the railway crossing on his way to visit a sick man. He wore his gun as usual, and, as it was a warm day, he removed his coat as he walked along. Just at the edge of town he met a man, a big stranger in a brown suit, wearing a large brown mustache. As their eyes met a slight shock seemed to pass through both men. Dan thought, "Here he is," and the stranger must have recognized a "tall man with curly hair" who wore a gun. They stood still, facing each other for a moment, then the stranger turned away and continued on his way into town. Dan waited quietly, then followed him, a few yards behind. The man kept looking back uneasily as they walked through the old part of town, and on to the hotel.

As the two men entered, Dan a few feet behind, the hotel manager looked up and caught Dan's signal. When the stranger asked for a room, Dan shook his head slightly and the manager said, "Sorry, stranger, but we haven't a room vacant. Better go back to Arizona's, he might have one."

Really uneasy now, the stranger asked where he could find this place, and the constable, who had seen both men enter the hotel, appeared at the man's side and answered him, "Back the way you came, along the main street to the big rooming house on the corner. Can't miss it. Come on, we'll walk back with you."

He and Dan walked on either side of the now decidedly nervous man, all the way to the rooming house. As they entered and walked up to the desk, several men watched the procession. When the stranger asked for a room, at a nod from the constable, Arizona picked up a rifle from under the desk, laying it on the counter while the stranger signed the register.

Arizona picked up the small suitcase, the man's only luggage, and led him upstairs to a room. After a few minutes, Dan and the constable went up to pay him a call. They searched his luggage but found no weapon, which was not surprising as the man was obviously only spying out the land. Then they told him, "We don't like your looks, especially your false mustache; you had better be on the train for the coast on Wednesday morning."

Throughout these proceedings, the man had not spoken, but when this sentence of banishment was pronounced, he blurted out, "You got nothin' on me!"

"And we don't want to have. That's why we're telling you to be on that train," he was told. "And while you are waiting for it, mind what you do, because we'll be keeping an eye on you." Then they left him sitting on the edge of his bed, glaring hatred at them.

Dan came home and ate his supper, making no mention of his afternoon adventure, but I was by this time the only person in the town who didn't know all about it. Later in the evening, I went to a neighbour's home and found several other women there. As I walked up the path, I could here them talking excitedly, but as soon as I appeared, they were silent. I was slightly puzzled, but as I was accustomed to having my every movement commented upon, I just wondered what I had been doing this time.

I stayed only a few minutes, since they were ill at ease in my presence, and walked over to the drug store. As soon as I entered I saw Alfie Bird, a small excitable cockney, hopping around like a drop of water on a hot stove. He recognized me and almost screamed, "Ee there! Ain't you scared to be abaht, now that 'ee's 'ere? I mean the one oo's come to kill yer 'usband!"

My blood seemed to turn to icewater and my throat closed up tight. After a minute I answered coolly, "He'll need to be pretty quick on the draw to beat Doc."

Just then the druggist appeared and scowled furiously at poor Alfie, who had no idea what he had done until I turned to leave the store. "You had better be sure Doc doesn't find out that you told me about our murderous friend, or there may be a new face in heaven in the morning. Yours!"

I closed the door, and walked as quickly as my shaking legs would carry me towards home. I hoped Alfie would survive his fright.

When I reached the cabin, my nonchalant Dan was at his desk beside the lamp, blinds wide open in spite of the constable's warning. I went around pulling them down. I was still frightened, but turned furiously on Dan when he asked me what I was doing. "Might be as well to take a few precautions as you were ordered to until your friend leaves town."

"Who told you?" It was Dan's turn to be angry.

I answered as airily as I could considering the butterflies in my stomach, "Oh, everyone is acting so peculiarly this evening; they stop talking when I appear, and they look at me so sympathetically. You might have told me yourself."

"If I find out who was so free with his information, I'll make him wish his mother had drowned him before his eyes were opened!" He added some choice expressions which were definitely unpreacherlike. (I understood his anger, because after all that had transpired, he was afraid of my finding out about it, adding to my worries.)

"If I told you who it was, it wouldn't do any good. I was bound to find out somehow, in this small place, when everyone else knew. So don't worry, I'll be all right, if you will only promise to be careful."

Wednesday morning the man was escorted to the station by most of the population, as everyone wanted to have a good look at him. I didn't go as I had seen him the day before, as he walked along the street. Dan called me to the back door and pointed to the man about a half block away.

"There he is, harmless as a dove. He hasn't made a move unseen since he arrived, and right now he wants only one thing, to get out of town, and back to the rest of his gang, wherever they are."

After the train left, the bandit tried to get off at each of the next three stops, only to discover that the man who sat next to him, whistling quietly to himself, was a plain clothes detective. He was promptly pushed back into his seat every time he stood up while the train was stopped. He was told, "This isn't your station, mister. You're going all the way to the coast to catch the next boat back to Seattle."

The avenging brother was gone, but so was my peace of mind. Everyone was glad to have him gone, but none so glad as I.

I was staying at home most of the time now as my baby was due within a few weeks. All the stress and worry of that summer had taxed my nervous system most severely. I worked and rested, ate and slept like an automaton, so quietly that my friends exclaimed at my self-control and wonderful courage, as they called it. If they had only known, I was numb.

When the evening came for my baby to be born, Dan went to the hotel to find the livery man, as he needed a horse and buggy to take me to the hospital. The hotel owner, Black Jack, heard him asking about a conveyance and hurried over to Dan, almost shouting, "Livery indeed! Isn't my Billy and the rubber-tired buggy good enough for you to take your wife to the hospital? When did the Doc have to hire a horse and buggy while I have the finest outfit in the country!"

Dan smiled and said, "Thanks, Jack, I'll take your horse and buggy gladly, but I didn't like to ask you for them."

"And why not? Billy'd be dead this minute if it weren't for you, and you can have him any time you want him, day or night. Come on, we'll hitch up."

Black Jack MacDonell was one of those characters to be found wherever a new district is to be opened up. He was known from San Francisco to Nome and the Yukon as the king of the saloon-keepers. He sold liquor and sponsored prostitutes in every part of the Pacific coast, and he had been heard to say that he would fire any honest man he found in his employ. In spite of his threat, he had many perfectly honest men working for him, at least as honest as it was possible to be in that business.

Jack had an enormous paunch, so I doubt if he could see his boots, much less tie them, but he was inordinately fond of it. Dan had asked him one time to take a hand on a tug-o'-war rope and Jack had roared indignantly, "It has cost me $50,000 to put on this bay window, and I'm not doing anything to hurt it, not me!"

He also loved horses, and Billy was the apple of his eye. He was a very fine horse and his owner took great care of him, watching his food, keeping him well-brushed, and exercising him regularly. Sometimes in the late autumn Jack would send the horse to pasture for a while on a ranch he owned about fifty miles east of Hazelton. Billy was a driving horse, so nobody was supposed to put a saddle on him. On one occasion, Dan was riding past a small village in the valley when he saw Billy, saddled, and tied to a post outside the hotel. It was a cold, rainy day, but it was payday and the ranch foreman had come in to cash his cheque. Since Black Jack owned the saloon, he expected his ranch hands to cash their cheques there and to spend them. The foreman was doing his best to comply.

Dan noticed that Billy was shivering from the cold, although it was evident that he had been sweating, so he telephoned Jack, telling him that he had better come up to collect his sick horse. He then went into the bar, took the foreman outside, and made him lead Billy back to the ranch immediately. Dan himself followed the man and the horse as he knew the horse was heading for pneumonia, and that he would need a great deal of care.

When Black Jack arrived, driven to the ranch by one of his friends, he found the battle for Billy's life was on in earnest. The horse was doctored and nursed by day and night, giving Dan time for only short naps between medicines. Finally, Billy began to take an interest in life once more, and he was soon out of danger. Black Jack tried to thank Dan, but all he could think of was the foreman who had caused the trouble. The man had been discharged as soon as Jack arrived.

"My God, Doc! He had strict orders never to ride Billy. He's a drivin' horse and then he goes and rides him and leaves him standin'." Jack cursed and cried, calling the foreman every name he knew, and he knew a great many, it seemed. After some ten minutes during which Dan vowed Jack did not repeat himself once, he stopped for breath. He looked at Dan with a face as innocent as a child and finished with, "You know, Doc, I believe in my heart that God will punish a man like that!"

Dan, who was almost speechless with inner laughter, agreed.

This was the explanation for the generous offer of the horse and buggy to take me to the hospital. No other person in the whole valley had been given the privilege of driving Billy, and this offer was the measure of the Jack's gratitude to Dan.

When it was time to bring me home again, Dan arrived at the hospital with not only Billy and the rubber-tired buggy, but a new laprobe and whip, bought in honour of the occasion.

Black Jack was like many of the so-called bad men of the frontier, a mixture of good and bad, violence and gentleness, dishonesty and generosity, but always a personality.

CHAPTER 21

A
Love
Story

WORLD WAR I HAD BEGUN, and before the end of 1914, nearly every young man in the town and surrounding country had enlisted and gone to training camp. It was quieter now than one could believe possible after the uproarious years of construction. But it had been the most frightening and unhappy year of my life. The agony of fear that had been mine since that dreadful April morning swept over me as though the birth of my baby had broken the flood gates, and I was submerged in terror.

The seventh robber was still at large, as far as we knew, although it was rumoured that he had been able to get back to Seattle, which was the gang's headquarters. This was unconfirmed however, and I couldn't believe it. He and his leader, bent on revenge, seemed to be close at hand all the time.

Every time Dan was out of my sight, I heard the deafening echo of gunfire, and I was uneasy until I heard his returning steps on the porch. I couldnot be left alone, so we persuaded my cousin Estelle to come from Ontario to take care of me. I was badly in need of sleep. The danger was real enough to Dan, and I knew he recognized it because he always kept his fully-loaded Colt .44 close to our bed. He slept, but I was unable to sleep for an hour while it was dark, and in the north there are many hours of darkness. Subconsciously, I felt that I must keep watch while he slept, until dawn lightened the day, when I would fall asleep for a few hours. In the night I would listen for every slightest sound until I had to feel my ears to make sure they weren't as big as a donkey's! It was always a relief to find them the usual size.

A night policeman had been engaged to patrol our end of the village, and Hazelton's new police chief, Alex Minty, a Canadian with several years' experience in the Northwest, had given his strict orders to keep our cabin under close watch. He did this, quite literally.

On the Sunday of Estelle's arrival, we sat talking after church until nearly midnight. After my cousin had retired, I was in bed and Dan was half undressed. There was no light in our room and we were tired and quiet. Then we heard a slight sound, like a step on the plank sidewalk, as of someone on tiptoe. Breathlessly we listened, and in the dim light from the window I saw Dan reach for his gun. As he picked it up there was a loud and heavy step, and a bright light flashed on the window. I think I lost consciousness for a second, but not Dan. Shoes unlaced, pulling up his braces as he ran, he left the cabin with lightning speed. He saw a dark figure hurrying down the street, and began to run faster as did the man ahead of him. For nearly half a mile the two men sped across shortcuts, down alleys and over logs until they reached the police station, where the pursued man burst through the doorway and collapsed on the floor. It was the night policeman. Dan prodded him with the muzzle of his gun.

"Get up and tell me what you were doing prowling around our cabin, and flashing a light on the window like that?"

"Gosh, Doc! I didn't mean to scare you, I'm the night policeman and I was just trying to do my job."

"I knew who you were the minute I saw you, but I thought it would be a good idea to teach you a lesson!"

The poor fellow was mumbling, "My God, Doc, I thought sure you were going to bore me."

"And you weren't far wrong, either. Of all the crazy things to do, to come creeping up to the window in the middle of the night and turn your flashlight on us! You nearly frightened my wife to death!"

Phil Meagher with Margaret at the Ore Rock, New Hazelton.

"She's got nothin' on me. I'm still scared!"

Lavery, the constable, walked out of the back room, and asked what all the noise was about. Dan told him in no uncertain terms.

"You're fired, you stupid ass! I told you distinctly not to go near the Doc's house, just keep an eye in that direction!"

"I'm not fired," he said, "I quit about a hundred yards from Doc's house. So would you if you'd had this long-legged two-gun cow puncher on your heels gainin' with every jump, and expectin' to have a bullet between your shoulder blades any minute. I haven't been the night policeman for the last ten minutes and you can have your job."

By this time, both Dan and Lavery were laughing at the frantic man, although to me it was no laughing matter.

During the winter that followed, our friend Phil Meagher, a retired Yukon miner, developed a taste for church services. I don't suppose he had gone to church since he was a boy, and his hair was white now. I had recovered my health to some extent, so we returned to an old practice of having a few friends in for coffee after the service and Phil became a regular visitor.

One evening as we sat with our coffee and cake, Phil was seized with a sudden desire to sneeze, and hastily pulled a handkerchief from his hip pocket. Out tumbled a business-like revolver, along with the handkerchief. We all stared, especially Estelle, who was horrified, and I could sense she was wondering what kind of man this was, with a gun in his suit pocket. Answering our questioning looks, Phil said almost shyly, "Well, Doc, I know you wear your gun under your Prince Albert, but you get sort of interested in your sermon and can't watch the windows. Thought I'd just toddle along and keep my eyes open."

Dan's arm was around Phil's shoulder by the time he finished his explanation, and there was moisture in his eyes as he said, "You old rascal! Now I know why everywhere I've been these last few months you were sure to turn up somewhere. You've been watching me like a nursemaid."

"Someone needs to watch you since you won't watch yourself. I'm older than you, and I don't trust anyone much, not even myself." His sudden taste for church-going was explained and the subject was never mentioned again. Even Estelle was awed into silence, though her thoughts must have been chaotic. Dan, with a gun under his Sunday coat, in church!

The glorious spring weather was healing my wounded spirit in spite of myself, and Dan and I were taking our evening walks again. One evening, we walked along our favourite trail to the top of the hill (all the towns in the North have hills behind them), and stood looking across the river to the hills beyond. There had been a bridge built across the Bulkley Canyon at Hagwilget, but I had not yet crossed it. Dan said, "Let's saddle up and ride across the bridge tomorrow. We'll take a picnic lunch and make a day of it. What do you say?"

"I'd love it, but it's so long since I rode Tim, he'll probably throw me over his head. But I'd risk even that for a picnic."

Tim was a former race horse from the south, and he was a real pleasure to ride. A bright chestnut in colour, Tim had only one failing — he always wanted to run. Fortunately, he wasn't hard to hold, and he had no other bad habits, unless he was frightened, and then he might, just possibly, buck a little.

The bridge which we were to cross was swung on cables across the narrowest part of the canyon and it was only nine feet wide. The water boiled and whirled more than three hundred feet below. Tim was in lively mood and I had to hold him in all the way to the bridge, in the centre of which was a metal plate carrying

First high level
bridge, built in
1913 during Dan
and Eva's
residence.
Another bridge
has been built
since.

the name of the cable company; this rattled noisily when anything passed it.
This time was no exception. When we reached the plate, Tim rolled his eyes,
stopped short, and put down his head. Fortunately, Dan was watching, and
he reached out quickly, seized Tim's bridle, and pulled his head up again. I
slipped off on the wrong side, away from the railing, which at this point was
only three feet high, and I walked the rest of the way across. There was an
excellent chance that if Dan hadn't seen what was coming, I would have gone
over Tim's head, and over the railing as well.

It was a long time before I stopped dreaming that I was falling, down, down
into that deep white water.

We enjoyed our picnic in spite of the incident, but on the return journey
we rode the long way around and crossed the river by the low-level bridge to
prevent a recurrence of the problem.

Our doctor had given orders that I was to spend every possible minute in
the open air. The new baby, Marian, was very little bother after she had her
morning bath and bottle, and Estelle proved to be a good nurse and housekeeper. My greatest problem was how to keep her with me, since she was the
only single woman in the village. She was besieged by the few young men who
were there, some of them on leave from the war, others waiting to be
transferred, and a few who were unable to go at all.

One young mining engineer, Roy Canfold, seemed to be her favourite escort, and before long her only companion. He had taken his officer's training at a university and he was soon to join his regiment at Vernon. From there he might be sent to the battle front any day. One day, Estelle told me that she had promised to marry him, if possible before he left for overseas.

We were pleased about the engagement as Roy was a young man of excellent character. He was tall and well built, not handsome of face, but very pleasant in his manner. Estelle's only regret was that she would not be able to marry him at home in Ontario, so she hesitated to carry through with her marriage plans.

I felt sure that Estelle's mother was responsible for this hesitation, and my cousin confirmed my suspicion one day when I found her crying over a letter.

"Eva, I'm so unhappy!" she sobbed.

"What's the matter Estelle, have you had bad news?" I asked.

"Yes, but not what you think. Eva, I feel like a monster sending Roy to war without marrying him, but just look at this letter from Mother," and she pushed the sheet of paper into my hand.

I read it and seethed with rage. Estelle's mother evidently did not want her to marry anyone without the family knowing all about him. She was twenty-three and did not require their consent, but she wanted it anyway. I read, "We could not endure the thought of your marrying a young man who had been exposed to the wild life of the North. You have been very carefully brought up and could not be expected to know the temptations to which young men are exposed in that lawless land. Of course, he may be all that you say he is, and I'm sure Eva and Dan would not encourage anyone but a respectable young man in their home. But really dear, you know they seem to have acquired some very peculiar ideas and I'm not entirely sure of their judgement. Please wait until after the war to be married and come home now to wait for Roy's return. Believe me, daughter, it is best that way."

Estelle's tears were dried, and her eyes shone with anger, matching the blaze in mine. Then I began to laugh. "Estelle, can you imagine that parents like ours, living all their lives in one place, could know so little of what goes on in the lives of others around them? If there weren't as much temptation in that little old town as anywhere on earth, I must have forgotten many of the things that happened there during my years in office work. There was a lot of hypocrisy hidden under a cloak of religion and respectability. One has to work with people through the week to really know them. Many of them were what our old friend Harry Davies used to call 'Sunday people.'"

"Eva, would you write mother and tell her what a grand guy Roy is? She might believe you."

I shook my head doubtfully. "I don't think it would do a bit of good. We have funny ideas, remember? Perhaps a better idea would be for me to write Father and ask him to see your folks and tell them how you feel. He has a better opinion of us than your mother has. I'll write him today, if you think it will help."

"Oh yes, Eva, please do. Uncle John would be the very one. Mother thinks the world of him, and maybe he could persuade her to be a little bit more understanding."

Writing my father was a good idea because just two weeks later Estelle received word that her parents would give their consent to her marriage whenever she wished. She was jubilant and wrote to Roy immediately. He answered at once saying he would have two weeks leave before sailing, they could be married then, and have a short honeymoon before he had to leave her. We began at once to prepare for the wedding, gathering as much of a trousseau as was possible in a short time. Then three weeks later Roy's wire came. "All leaves cancelled."

The letter arrived and it said, "Maybe it's better this way, because when I get back, and I'm sure I will, we can be married in your home as your parents wish. Keep your courage up darling, and write as often as you can. As soon as we have chased the Germans back across the Rhine, I'll come home to you. Give my love to Eva and Dan and thank them for being so kind to us . . . ."

Exactly one month from the day Roy sailed from Halifax, he was killed in action. Estelle changed in a few short weeks from a laughing, happy person to an older, sadder woman. Her lovely brown hair was dull from lack of care, her eyes faded from crying, and she ate so little she lost a great deal of weight. She was beginning to look like a shadow when she finally decided to go home.

"I don't care about anything, Eva, so I might as well be there as here. Maybe I can blot out these months somehow, and start over. But I can't forgive my mother for what she said about Roy's death. I didn't tell you because I was ashamed, but Mother said it was probably all for the best as he might have come home crippled or disfigured and I would be tied to him for the rest of my life, and not get married again. Can you believe such a cruel thing?"

I couldn't, but when she showed me the letter, it left me speechless.

"Why do we have to have wars, anyway, Eva?"

"That's what a great many of us are asking, and we're not finding an answer, Estelle," I said. "The boys who have to do the fighting and dying certainly aren't the ones to make war. They just have to fight it. I'm hoping that some day only the ones who make quarrels have to do the fighting. Then those armchair generals, and pot-bellied tycoons who make money out of war, would soon find a way to stop it! They don't die in the trenches and leave loved ones at home to face poverty and loneliness, perhaps for the rest of their lives!"

"If you said a thing like that at home, Eva, they'd put you in jail or maybe stone you. But they're going to hear it from me!" Estelle's chin came up and her eyeflashed with some of her old spirit.

And so she went home, and her departure left me lonely, but not for long. The war was well underway, and I was swept up in a whirlwind of Red Cross and Belgian Relief drives. The people thought they ought to raise money for these causes and decided to hold a series of dances.

There was just one obstacle. There was no music for dancing, except a few scratchy records for the gramophones that might be found. Then someone had a bright idea, and I was asked if I would play the piano for them. There was one man, a surveyor named Affleck, who had a piano, and he offered to have it brought down to the hall, if I would play for the dancers. Churchgoers had always thought it sinful for a minister's wife to play for dancing, but now the war made everything right. As for me, war or no war, I was delighted to have the opportunity. Dancing had been one of my favourite pastimes before I was married, second only to playing for dancing.

So, I offered my services as my contribution to the war effort, and they were accepted with wild enthusiasm. The newcomers to the North were the only ones who had ever had any objection to such a scheme, and now they were all for it. The old-timers had never had any doubt about the matter. To them dancing was a good wholesome recreation, and I was just "Doc's wife," so they had no particular set of rules for my behaviour.

I played many hours that winter and my performances were the best thing that could have happened to me, because they took my mind off my own troubles and I ceased lying awake at night, waiting for daylight and sleep.

CHAPTER 22

The
Changing
Scene

THE WAR AND THE DEPARTING YOUNG MEN were only part of the changing scene. One by one the old roadhouses closed, landmarks disappeared, and civilization crept over the Skeena Valley. The trains went dashing through from coast to coast, bringing mail, passengers and freight. When the train unloaded at the station it looked drab and uninteresting.

Life had been more colourful when everyone in town stood shoulder to shoulder on the wharf listening to the chug-chug-chug of the riverboat puffing its way up the river; when we ran out into the road to watch the barking dogs galloping by with sleds piled with bags of mail in the wintertime.

The friendly little towns became impersonal, merely stations on a transcontinental railway. The men and women of those towns were just people watching the trains go by. The Skeena Valley seemed to have lost its glowing personality altogether. Those who had spent their years pioneering in one place or another were looking for new worlds to conquer or new roads to build.

The sad part was that for them, and their methods, the North had been the last great Canadian frontier. After World War I, motor transport, planes, radios, new and improved machinery, and other scientific discoveries, made it impossible for any place in this country to be as isolated as was the Skeena Valley before the railroad's arrival. On any new construction project, none of

Main Street, New Hazelton, circa 1914.

the old methods were used, no hand scrapers, picks and shovels, horses and mules, or great freight wagons. Work would not be done by hand, but by machines in the hands of younger men trained in their use.

Daily communication with the outer world kept everyone in touch with the world's events; planes carried mail from any part of Canada or the United States in less time than it would take the stage or dog team to cover fifty miles.

There seemed nothing left for the older pioneers but to exchange their whipcords and riding boots for overalls, settle for a piece of land, start a store, or some other business in one of the little towns that were springing up all along the railroad and highways. Prospectors with the search for gold or other precious metals in their blood, and the wild free life in their hearts, scanned the mining news for scent of a strike, somewhere, anywhere, just a strike!

To add to the desolation, the Hudson's Bay trading post burned one night. Warehouse, store, and living quarters — all were gone. Those whitewashed log buildings were part of the whole north country and they belonged to the days of the pioneers.

It was late in the evening when the triangle fire gong rang out in the Old Town; although many had already retired, it was a signal nobody ignored, as every able-bodied man in town belonged to the volunteer fire brigade. It meant something to be a fire fighter, too, for the water had to be handed up a human chain, pail by pail from the river to the burning building. The chain was formed quickly, as the Hudson's Bay buildings were right on the river bank.

In a very short time a large crowd had assembled and the excitement was intense. The buildings were old and dry, and there was little chance of saving them, so the men concentrated on removing some of the goods to safety.

Closest to the river was a smaller building around which some men were clustered, and a watching stranger came to the conclusion this must be where the papers and more expensive furs were kept, like a large vault. The parcels which were being handed out were a peculiar shape for furs or papers, he thought. He told us afterwards, "Up there, against a background of flame, a row of men sat a stride the peak of this building. They emptied buckets of water with one hand, while with the other they clutched small parcels to their bosoms. Gallons and gallons of water they poured over the stone walls of that small building, and when the flames from the fire faded, one old-timer in a strangely thickened voice called down, 'Sall right boysh!' as he placed his hand on the fireproof slates of the roof, 'Danger's past! It's shafe.'"

The stranger continued, "With shouts of triumph, they raised their arms, every man perched there, and silhouetted against that pale glow, they lifted bottles to their lips, and tipping their heads back for all the world like a band of trumpeters about to sound a fanfare, they swallowed the few remaining drops." He paused, then added, "They had saved the wine cellar!"

Other landmarks were disappearing, one by one. Shortly after the fire, Dan rode out to one of the valley ranches to treat an injured horse. He drank in the clear, sweet spring air while his mind was busy with memories of the exciting days of the past four years. He later told me he was feeling rather low at the thought of leaving the North at the end of June.

As he rounded a bend in the road he saw a band of horses grazing in a nearby field. He recognized them at once as the Cataline packtrain, turned out to grass.

"You know, Eve, there was a feeling of shock, a sort of nostalgia swept over

Cataline Packtrain in Hudson's Bay Co. corral. Well known for herding cattle from central B.C. to the north country, supplying fresh meat to small communities along the way.

me when I recognized the old Cataline packtrain. Like a picture of the old ways I saw passing, the packtrains, the dog teams, Yukon sleds, six-horse freight wagons, and all the ways of the pioneers being pushed aside by the encroaching world."

"Well, Dan," I said, "progress is good and necessary, isn't it?"

"Yes, I suppose so, but . . . ." Dan fell silent again, his thoughts busy with tales of that old packtrain so well known for fifty years both in the Interior to the south, and in northern British Columbia.

Jean Cataline was a strange mixture of origin. He claimed to be of Mexican, Native, French, and Spanish birth, and he was unique both in appearance and character. He seemed to have no family, or at least never spoke of one; his friends were few, and his acquaintances many, which was the way he wanted it. His fiery temper and most peculiar habits did not endear him to many people, but his horses, or his "ponees" as he called them, didn't seem to mind at all. They were his family, and his life had been spent with his "ponees" up to the time he had retired and turned them out to grass. Cataline was a small man physically, but his fierce black eyes, the luxuriant black hair which hung down to his shoulders, and his extremely vivid personality made him seem formidable. One of his habits, well-known when he came in from a long trip, was to buy a bottle of rum, drink half of it, and pour the rest on his hair. This met with a good deal of resentment from other men, who couldn't bear to see good liquor wasted on anybody's hair. Cataline explained why he did it, quite aptly, "Thees rum, if she's good for my inside, she's good for my hair."

Dan remembered well the day when, accompanied by the police chief, he went to the corral where the packtrain was being loaded for a trip to the mountains. Dan had noticed that some of the horses had running sores, or fistulas, on their shoulders. These sores were caused by careless packing. When the saddles were loosely tied, they would slip backwards on the upgrades and forward on the downhill trails. The constant friction broke the skin, and dirt and dust gathered to complete the wound. He had spoken about it to the chief, who decided to ask Cataline to take these affected horses out of the train for a few days so their wounds might heal.

When the chief told Cataline the horses must be unpacked and left behind, the angered man tore his hair, cursed in his native languages as well as in English, and finally brandished a long knife which he carried for scaring purposes only. It seems unlikely he would have used it under ordinary circumstances, but he usually didn't need to as its sight and the sound of the old man's shouts were more than enough to frighten most people.

When Dan promised to cure his ponies as quickly as possible, the matter was amicably settled. Cataline didn't really want to hurt his ponies, he was just careless in such matters.

After his packtrain was no longer needed, and his ponies had been turned out to pasture, Cataline's health failed rapidly. His work was gone and he retired to a cabin at Kispiox where he soon became so ill he had to be taken to a hospital; there he died not long afterwards. He didn't seem to want to live without his "ponees" and made little effort to do so.

Shortly before his death Cataline said to the nurse who was bending over his bed, "Well, nurse, ole Cataline, he's goin' to die, eh?"

"Now Cataline, you mustn't talk like that!" she answered. "We're taking good care of you, and we'll have you on your feet again before long."

"No, thees time I leave my poor ponees for keeps. They'll miss ole Cataline."

Tears filled his eyes, which had lost all their fierce gleam, and the nurse found tears were not far from her own eyes as she thought pityingly of the poor old man dying all alone, with no one of his own near him. She said gently, "Now you must sleep. Let me fix your pillow." As she bent over the bed, Cataline looked up at her and said, "Nurse, when I get up dere to Heaven, you think maybe the good padre, maybe he let me have wan leetle ponee? What you say?"

The nurse put her hand gently on his shoulder and answered, "Sure he will, Cataline. I know he will!"

Satisfied, the old king of the packers went quietly to sleep. He died the next day without speaking again. The nurse cried when she told the others the story, but she was glad she had given him enough hope to make his last hours a little happier. Those who had known him a long time, however, wondered what effect the old warrior would have on the kind of Heaven the Bible tells about, if something didn't happen to suit him. Particularly if he didn't get his "ponee!"

CHAPTER 23

A
Prospector's
Tale

NEW HAZELTON WAS FAST BECOMING A GHOST TOWN. The streets were so silent it was impossible to believe that such a short time ago they had been throbbing with life, as the swings of six and eight-horse teams with their heavily laden wagons had rolled through the valley in continuous streams; crowds of men surging through the streets, and every poolroom, café, and stopping place filled to overflowing. It was too quiet for Dan. He was yearning for new places and more challenge. Living intensely every hour of the day for years, at a high emotional pitch, had a tendency to make tranquility humdrum and unbearable.

My reaction was somewhat different. At the moment, I felt I had experienced enough excitement to last a lifetime. I was still suffering from shattered nerves, and was longing for some of that tranquility, even if it was humdrum.

Dan received a call to a church in Quesnel in the heart of the upper Cariboo country, and he decided to have a look at the place before accepting the offer. I was hardly well enough to be left alone with two children, and wished for some congenial person to stay with me during his absence. My wish was answered when I received a letter from Vancouver sent by my friend, Marie.

"I'm coming to Hazelton for a few days to see some people about a mining

195

prospect that Harry Davies left me," she wrote. "I have an offer to sell it and have decided to accept. You will see me soon, perhaps next week, and I'm looking forward to a visit with you and your family."

I wrote to her by return mail, inviting her to stay with me for the ten days that Dan would be away and she answered affirmatively by return mail. She would love to stay with me and she would arrive by Thursday's train. I thought my troubles were over, but I discovered that a few townswomen thought Marie quite unsuitable for me to have as my guest. My real friends assured me that my visitors were none of their business, so I closed my ears to the unkind remarks. We were leaving Hazelton anyway, so I let them talk without defending myself.

Marie arrived, looking serene and happy, and just as helpful and forthright as usual. She cleaned the cabin for me, helped with the packing, and adored the children. In fact, she spoiled them outrageously. She was a born mother with no one of her own to care for, so she poured out her love on other children. She had done well for herself with her rooming house, and had made a place for herself in spite of the unhappy years of the past. Marie was one of the kindliest souls I have ever known, and she taught me much.

Dan returned the day after she left, and he regretted having missed her, but he was so thrilled and excited about the wonderful country he had been visiting that he couldn't stop talking about it. One evening, in the midst of his description of the Cariboo country, he said suddenly, "Do you remember the story Harry told us about the pail on the tree on the Cariboo highway?"

"Yes, I remember! Did you see it?"

"I not only saw it, but I met the old man who put it there. He told me the whole story. Want to hear it?"

"I'll put the coffee pot on and we can pretend that Harry is here to drink it with us."

"When I decided to make the round trip home through Ashcroft, Vancouver, and Prince Rupert," he began, "I booked a seat on the stage from Quesnel. There was only one other passenger, and he turned out to be Jim Cummings, the man Harry told us was one of the thousands who went to Barkerville in the 1860s, so he was getting pretty old, and had to go down to Ashcroft to the hospital for treatment.

"We bumped along over an incredibly rough road until we came to a place called Steamboat Landing. Just as we reached this spot, Jim leaned forward and asked the driver to stop the stage for a minute as he wanted to get out. I followed him because he looked awfully sick and feeble. But he wasn't sick, he just wanted to stop and take a look at a tree which stood at the side of the road. It was a tall fir, about sixteen inches through at the butt. Jim was pointing upward at a black band around the tree about thirty feet up; a circular piece of black metal hung down from the edge of the pail.

"Jim stood and gazed as though he couldn't believe his eyes. 'There it is! As sure as life there it is! Sure as my name is Jim Cummings!' He shook his head with wonder in his voice, 'I can't believe it!'

"'What is it?' I asked, although by this time I knew it must be the pail.

"'A pail,' said Jim, and he chuckled with reminiscent glee. 'I stuck it there when I come this way in the early sixties, and now I'm seein' it again for the first time in over fifty years. The fellows told me it was still there but I didn't believe it — thought they were joking.'" Dan took a sip of coffee and went on, "The driver was shouting impatiently as he wanted to be on his way. The horses were fresh, having just taken over a few miles back at the stage stables. As soon as we were in our seats he drove on, at a gallop, as if to make up for lost time. After a few minutes Jim began to talk. He had started up the road for the Cariboo gold fields in the spring of 1860, with three other fellows, he told me, so I asked if one of them was Harry Davies. Jim was surprised that we knew Harry, but, as I explained, Harry had been one of our greatest friends in Hazelton. I told Jim that Harry had left Barkerville, that he went into Manson Creek about 1870; when we knew him, he was living in Hazelton along with several other retired prospectors. Of course, Jim wanted to know if Harry had told us about him."

Dan recounted Harry's version of the trip to Barkerville to Jim, telling him that Harry had mentioned the pail and the tree. At that, Jim chuckled and then began to tell his story to Dan.

"We took the boat to Yale, as far as it went in those days, then we tramped the rest of the way. Slept wherever night found us, panned a little gold out of the sand bars of the Fraser, had a few set-tos with the Natives, but kept right on goin' north.

"It was fall when we got along this far and it was dashed cold the night we camped here at Steamboat Landing. It was sure chilly that night, and in the morning we didn't waste any time gettin' a fire goin' and the tea pail on. That bucket you were lookin' at back there was the very one we hung over the fire that morning. We huddled around the fire tryin' to get warm and waitin' for the water to boil, when all at once the pesky pail sprung a leak and the water ran down all over the fire and blame near put it out. I was so all-fired mad I just grabbed it off the hook and put my foot right through the bottom and tore it off near all the way round. 'So,' says I, 'you would spring a leak just when we needed you most! Then here's where you stay till you rot!' And by Gad, I turned it upside down and pulled it down over the end of a fir sapling and left it."

Jim's laugh was pretty shaky, and he sat lost in thought while the stage moved along for a mile or so, Dan told me. Then he had said, softly, "Here I am, past eighty, goin' back where I come from, and that old pail's still on the tree where I put it!"

"There were tears in his eyes and I wasn't a bit surprised," Dan told me. "He was old and weak, and badly stirred up at the sight of the pail. He sat still, looking straight ahead for a little while, then he turned in his seat and looked long toward the north. He seemed to be looking backward through all the years that had passed since that night at Steamboat Landing, right down the trail to this day, as he passed by on his way out of the north he loved, perhaps never to return. It was like someone turning in the doorway, looking back to say a last good-bye."

Dan and I sat silent, drinking our coffee, which had grown cold while Dan told this story. It was not until we had seen the Barkerville mining camp that we learned to what he had been saying his farewell.

It was good-bye to a log cabin which had been home to him for most of his lifetime. Good-bye to the clear, cool mornings when he hurried out to his claim, working long hours in the summertime to compensate for the long winters in Barkerville, when all the land lay deep in snow.

Good-bye to the gentle, roaring sounds of the mountain streams as they flowed swiftly through those gravel beds so richly dotted with gold; to the clink of the picks and shovels and the gentle swishing of water in the gold pans. Good-bye to Barkerville and its quaint cabins built on stilts to protect them from the spring freshets and the sand from the placer mining; to its fifteen thousand souls, all trying to get rich in one way or another; the tragedies which struck down so many as they fought their way to success or failure; the hardships and cold when their world was shut in by ice and snow.

It was good-bye to the vivid beauty of blue Jack-O-Clubs Lake.

And to the nights when darkness fell early and all those strong young men, abounding with life, made their way to the old opera house, dance hall, and saloon nearby, where they drank, and danced, and sang the night away; to the little piano which made music for the miners' and their "gals'" dancing feet away back in the days when the fir tree was still a sapling.

A last farewell to memories of the years when the blood ran more slowly and the town grew small as the mines closed one by one; when his hair turned gray, and he lived alone in the cabin in the town which was now just a ghost of its former self. Good-bye to old friends who passed silently away, one by one, leaving him lonely and old, and travelling swiftly toward the end of his own story.

Dan broke the silence. "You remember me mentioning the little piano. Well, you just ought to see it. It's sitting in the corner of the parlour in the Barkerville hotel. They say it was brought into the country on the back of a mule. It could have been, it's such a tiny thing. Now there isn't an ivory left on the keys. When I saw it there, huddled in the corner, a white scarf over the top, it made me think of some little old lady sitting in the chimney corner waiting for the great master-of-ceremonies to call the measures of the last quadrille."

Shortly afterwards we heard that Jim Cummings had passed away in the nursing home in Ashcroft.

CHAPTER 24

Farewells
and
Remembrances

Our sojourn in the green valley of the Skeena was almost over and in our hearts was an aching reluctance to leave. Perhaps it was because Hazelton was our first home, and although we had only a tent, we loved the place and would never forget it.

There were so many things to remember: the clear, blue sky; the sunshine and moonlight, both brighter because of the clean, smokeless air; the massive hills with their snowy crowns; the rushing rivers; and the jackpines.

We thought of all the friends we had made — prospectors, traders, trappers, and Natives, and many other folks who carried on the frontier's business life. We remembered the packtrains of ponies and dogs, the bustle of springtime when the trappers were coming in from the woods and the prospectors were hurrying out to their claims, the first boat puffing its way up the swift waters of the Skeena. We thought of the mail brought by dog teams in the winter, and their joyous barking as they came into town. These were sights we would never see again. We even forgot how those same dogs could howl in the night when we wanted to sleep.

But some things we would not forget so easily. The bank robbery had left an indelible memory for the people of Hazelton. The intruders were not men of the western world, but refugees from an old European civilization who knew

Larry Warner, a friend of Dan and
Eva, who later published a
newspaper in Smithers.

very little of the spirit of the Canadian North. A case in point for example, was
New Hazelton's George Montgomery, said to be the last surviving member of the
infamous Soapy Smith gang, who had terrorized the Yukon in Gold Rush days.
He was now a harmless little man, followed always by several dogs who found in
him a kind friend. The pioneers were for the most part honest and kindly, but the
men who came to rob the bank that April morning were a different breed, and
their punishment for breaking the rules followed without hesitation.

The day for our departure arrived. We had very little furniture to take with
us, and what we had was crated, our clothes and linen all packed, and Dan's
precious books crowded into boxes. We were to have dinner with Christina
and spend the evening with close friends. We set out early to make a little
farewell tour and found ourselves where we had so often been before, sitting
on a log on the brow of the hill to watch the late sunset. We thought about
our days in the North, and Dan remarked, "Isn't it strange, when you come
to think of it, most of our best friends are people who have never attended

church — Black Jack, Harry Davies, and oh yes, there's Jim May. What a great old boy he is! I'm sure he is the 'Tennessee Jim' Harry spoke of as being such a wise person."

We used to see Jim wander down past our tent twice a day, winter and summer, leaning on his staff, which was as long as he was, returning an hour or so later.

According to John Boyd, manager of the Hudson's Bay post, Jim and his partner prospected for many years in the Manson Creek area, and the post grub-staked them. They paid what they could, but were still owing quite a sum when Jim's partner died. Shortly afterward Jim found the gold he had been looking for all those years. It wasn't a rich claim, but he sold it for enough to take care of him for the rest of his life. The first thing he did was pay his debt, Boyd said. And although he didn't have to pay his partner's debt, he insisted, saying it was his sacred duty. "So we told him," Boyd went on, " that as long as he lived he would have his two glasses of rum every day. He comes down and sits in that arm chair, sips it slowly, and then goes home."

One day Dan asked him why he was so fond of rum, and he raised his glass, savoured the liquor's rich colour, and replied, "Some folks say bread is the staff of life, but this, ah, this is life itself!"

Jim was one of the few men legally married to a Native wife. Mary was a chief's daughter, and she and Jim were married in a traditional Native ceremony, as binding as though it had been blessed by a bishop. When some of the men asked him why he didn't send her back to her tribe as others had done, he answered sharply, "Mary was good to me when we were young and the going was rough. She's my wife and the mother of my son, and she'll stay my wife till the day I die."

It was no wonder he was called the "Mayor of Manson." He was known to be a wise man, plain-spoken and down-to-earth in his thinking. With the nearest policeman or judge a hundred miles away, he was usually called upon to settle quarrels and disputes over claims, women, equipment, or fights that started just to liven things up a bit. Jim would take a plug of tobacco from his pocket and bite off a chunk. He'd listen to both sides of the argument, then ponder and chew for a while. When he'd start turning his head from side to side and looking at the ground, the men would all jump back from him for safety. John Boyd had laughed when he told us of such an occasion.

"As soon as he had unloaded the tobacco juice he was ready to talk. Didn't say much, just seemed to be looking right through them and reading their minds, searching for the reasons behind all the fuss. Then he would say what he thought and leave it to the men themselves to decide what to do. His slow, Tennessee drawl cooled them down considerably. Then he'd walk away, and the fight was usually over." Of course, John added, "It might be the fact that Jim was six foot four inches in his stocking feet, with the strength of a grizzly bear in his arms, that had something to do with the respect they felt for his words."

As we continued our stroll, Charlie from the cookhouse came running towards us, worried lest he would not have a chance to say good-bye to us, "my good friends." Dan assured him we had planned to drop by and see him, recalling the many times Charlie had made coffee and sandwiches for him when he was called up the line at night. Then there were the times he had appeared at the tent door in the morning bringing part of a roasted chicken or a cake which he said were left over from a party, and were "all paid for, and someone must eat."

Charlie, in turn, reminded us of a time when Dan had done something for him, and had refused to be paid, but suggested that Charlie do something to help another fellow. So Charlie said, "Now all the time I try to do something good for the other fellow when he in trouble."

We shook hands with him and wished him good luck as long as he lived.

Dan's thoughts as Charlie returned the way he had come turned to the railroad, and the men with whom he came into daily contact in his work as a veterinarian. They came from all over Europe, the United States, and Canada. He valued the comradeship they shared. "They didn't owe me a thing, but they treated me like a brother, even when I scolded them, or tried to teach them to be more careful of themselves." He raised his hand to show the gold nugget ring on his finger, given to him by 'the boys.' "I wouldn't part with this for a fortune."

The train station in New
Hazelton. Eva on the right
beside friend Larry Warner,
newspaperman.

I reminded him that he had returned their friendship, when there was a sore
to be healed or a sliver to be removed. "They said they would rather have you
do it than one of the company doctors, because you boil your instruments,
and some of them just wipe them on their pants."

Dan agreed, "I know, I've seen them do it."

We looked across the canyon at the village of Hagwilget. "These years have
certainly been worthwhile for us, Eve. We've learned a lot about people which
I hope we won't forget." Dan said. He looked at his watch and stood up. I
stood beside him for a long minute as we took one last glance at the beautiful
scene, then turned back down the trail. I felt like laughing when I thought we
were the people who were to bring enlightenment to the people of the "far
land where sin doth abound and Satan lifteth up his head . . . ."

We were the ones who had been enlightened.

Then it was time to hurry back to Christina's for dinner.

It was late before we retired that night. Quite a crowd had gathered by the time we returned from our walk. Peggy sang for us, but I found I couldn't sing at all. There was a lump the size of an egg in my throat, so I just played for the others.

In the morning, we arrived at the station to find most of the town waiting to bid us good-bye. The train moved slowly away and we waved from the steps as they wished us a safe journey. We felt like a pair of lost souls.

The train was moving eastward but our thoughts were travelling back to the home we were leaving. We have relived every day of those years many times. When we arrived by river boat at the old town of Hazelton, we saw a land that was remote and primitive, but throbbing with beauty, violence, romance, and hardships.

The coming of the railway changed all that. It came with a vast array of men, shovels both large and small, dynamite, freight wagons and their skinners, horses and mules. The steel rails crept along the grade from the east to west, and west to east, coming closer and closer together until the day when they met, and the great transcontinental railway was completed.

At its coming, the quiet moonlight seemed to change suddenly from its soft tones to glaring neon lights; and brass bands blared and the circus came to town. For a while there was pandemonium, then at last the circus was over, the band packed up its instruments, the lights faded, animals and acrobats disappeared, tents were folded, and the wagons stole away.

Again, it was a remote land, green and still.

I seemed to hear once again the dean's voice saying, "You will be learning lessons as long as you live, each day will bring new experiences . . . ." How much wiser were his words than those of the minister who so harshly condemned the "far land" as a place of sin and Satan. Our horizons had widened considerably, our judgements were wiser and more understanding and our hearts were warmer towards our fellowmen than before we came to this land on our mission.

Now we were moving on to the Cariboo country in the northern interior of British Columbia, to our new home in Quesnel. The Barkerville gold fields of the sixties were about sixty miles eastward, and we would see this historic area as a ghost of its former self. There was no doubt our lessons in living would continue there, and we would try to learn them well.

The years since World War I have seen great changes in all parts of Canada. In Ontario, there were many farms like ours, with fields of grain and green grasses, well-cultivated gardens, and a variety of birds and animals. There were families in the homes.

There has been rapid growth in the programme of progress, and the fields and gardens are fast disappearing with the advent of housing developments, as the cities spread their wings ever wider. There are freeways and thousands of cars; there are airports and shopping centres, schools and the inevitable gas stations. Along the banks of the St. Mary's River great industries now belch their smoke and smells across that beautiful farming countryside, once fragrant with the scent of sweet clover. The river is no longer clear and sparkling.

In the northern valleys of the Skeena and Bulkley Rivers, there has been much of the same kind of transformation. Gone are the days of the pack ponies, sled dogs, miners and prospectors buying picks, shovels and gold pans at the trading posts. The residents use more sophisticated tools now.

It was an honest land, with an atmosphere of good fellowship, and a much kindlier tolerance and understanding shown to the weak and unfortunate than in the modern world. Helpful hands were always offered when they were needed, and peace was shattered only by influences from the outside world.

Now there are planes and trains, big business with its mills and industries, gas and oil operations, and paved highways where once there were only rugged trails. But in that north, a gleam of hope stirs in the hearts of our Native Canadians, which is giving them courage to fight for that which is their rightful heritage.

Those early days live forever in our minds and hearts, and as I have written earlier, one may love the Northland, or one may hate it, but it is impossible to forget.

Index

& Stewart boats 84; freighting
alcohol vs food 74, 104-106;
Hazelton riverboat 1, 24-27, 84;
Inlander riverboat 84; nostalgia for
189, 200; Port Simpson riverboat
25, 27-33, 84; Prince George
Steamer 19-20; tying up at bridge
123;
Boyd, John 202-203
Britain, see England
Bruce County (Ont.) 2
Buddhists 132
Bulkley Canyon 122-123, 183
Bulkley River xi, 35, 42, 123, 168
Bulkley Valley 26, 206
Burnaby viii
Burns, Pat 52, 136
"Cactus Jack" 117-118, 120
Camel train 118
Campbell-Johnson survey party 112
Canfold, Roy 185-186
Cariboo region 46, 49, 52, 195-197,
197, 206
Carman, Bliss (writer) 6
Carrier (natives) 56, 150
Cars, see Automobiles
Cascade Mountains 19
Cataline, Jean (Cataline packtrain)
191-194
Catholics 123, 142
Charleson's Lake 99, 101
Chase, Andy 87-88, 140-141
Chilcotin district 52, 136
Chinese 25, 107-108, 115, 131-132

Chippewas (natives) 9, 56
Christmas 6, 61, 83, 89, 91, 94-98, 101,
151
Clinton 118
Coast Range Mountains 19
Conservative Party 49
Conveyor (riverboat) 84
Copper mining 30-32
Cree (natives) 56
Crime, see Bank robberies, Police
Crowsnest Pass 16
Cummings, Jim 196-199
Cunningham (trading post operator)
45
Dalhousie University 12, 22
Dancing 9, 13, 101; dance halls 38, 45,
66, 79, 151; native dancing 60-61;
war relief dances 187-188
Davies, Harry 46-48, 74-77, 86,
97-98, 131, 151-152, 186, 196-197, 202
Dawson City (Yukon) 35, 66, 79
Devlin, Mrs. ("Dolly Louise") 66, 68
Distributor (riverboat) 84
Dillon, Matt 17
Dogs 38-39, 44, 67, 72-73, 83-90, 100,
126, 140-142, 145, 163, 189-190, 192,
200-201
Du Vernet (archbishop) 37-39
Duncan Ross Tunnel & Camp 153-154
Eaton (company) 7, 108
Edmonton (Alta.) 26
Education, school 3; business college
9-11; Dalhousie University 12, 22;
Knox College 12, 14; McGill

208